1979

University of St. Francis

W9-ACF-820

3 0301 00015808 5

John Russell

Copyright © 1970, 1972 by Roger C. Storms

Printed in the United States of America

PARTISAN PROPHETS

A History of the Prohibition Party, 1854-1972

By

Roger C. Storms

National Prohibition Foundation, Inc.
Post Office Box 2635
Denver, Colorado 80201

1972

LIBRARY
College of St. Francis
JOLIET, ILL.

SPONSORS

Our sincere thanks go to the individuals and organizations whose financial sponsorship of this book made its publication possible.

MR. EARL F. DODGE — Colorado

MR. JAMES HEDGES — Maryland

MR. CARROLL P. LAHMAN — Illinois

MR. WARREN N. McINTYRE — Pennsylvania

MAINE PROHIBITION COMMITTEE

PROHIBITION NATIONAL COMMITTEE

PARTISAN PROHIBITION HISTORICAL SOCIETY

PROHIBITION TRUST FUND

L.C. #73-152537

329.894
β 886

FOREWORD

The information on the following pages is the product of twelve years of study on the part of the author. It began as a curiosity, grew into a hobby, and now hopefully has evolved into a serious work. Much of the information contained herein comes from standard reference books, for very little has been written anywhere on the Prohibition Party as such. Indeed, very little has been written about the people in the movement. And even when it is, historians usually offer very little information on their place in the Prohibition Party.

One notable exception is Dr. Mary Earhart's biography, **Frances Willard,** which I commend to the serious student of political activism. Any party history owes a deep debt of gratitude to D. Leigh Colvin's book, **Prohibition in the United States.** While it contains much information on the temperance movement as a whole, it is the standard source of scholarly information on the party up to 1926. For the party's annals since that time, I have had to rely upon various periodicals and publications of the Prohibition National Committee, as well as the personal recollections of various individuals. A summer was spent in 1968 at the party's national headquarters in Kalazamoo, Michigan, during which time a good deal of information was gathered. I have sought to apply current historical discoveries and interpretations to this information in order to assess the place of the Prohibition Party in American history.

I have found that there have been three distinct periods in the party's development. I refer to these periods as: (1) the Prophetic period, 1854-1896; (2) the Pragmatic period, 1896-1932; (3) and the Fundamentalist period, 1932-1972. During the earliest years of the party, its leaders used a style similar to the Old Testament prophets. They envisioned an evangelistic transformation of America through which the party itself would remake the social order. Two lasting contributions were made which gave the Prohibition Party a great importance to American development. First of all, thousands of women were mobilized into the political process for the first time. The major parties and other third parties did not miss the point that women could be a powerful political force. The second important contribution was the fact that party leaders came from the most affluent colleges and congregations of the Northeast. This section of the country was the one most insulated against the Greenback and Populist reform movements. Only the Prohibition Party was organized to campaign successfully for reform in these areas.

The pragmatic period was a time when party leaders generally did not envision replacing one of the major parties. Their chief aim became one of pressure politics. They joined in coalitions with other organizations, hoping to infiltrate other temperance groups. Usually the reverse proved to be the final result. The greatest contribution of this period was activation of college students into a mass political movement for the first time in American history.

After 1932, smaller splinter groups within Protestantism began to assert themselves. These groups had been in the party for a long time, but had never assumed much leadership above the local level. More and more, there was a hardening against a name change that would bring in new groups. More and more the emphasis was placed on remaining righteous by keeping separate from an unclean political process. These were plainer, simpler people who were often suspicious of glamorous leaders with national reputations. The most important contribution of the

88375

party in this period was that of bringing these people into the political process. Many of them belonged to churches which had largely urged their people to abstain from worldly politics in the past. Now they were participating in an ecumenical effort with other denominations. Their children and grandchildren would find it that much easier to move on into the two-party system. The Prohibition Party did its share to build a national image for the fundamentalist movement, a movement that had previously felt alienated by the changes coming to modern American society. In so doing, the party helped to consolidate and institutionalize fundamentalism as a permanent force in the United States.

Much of this book is biographical. It is a story of partisan prophets. I tell their story because they are men who are being rapidly forgotten.

ABOUT THE AUTHOR

Roger C. Storms was born in 1939 at Houlton, Maine. He was educated in the public schools of Houlton, Gardiner, and Yarmouth, while his father was serving pastorates for the United Baptist Convention of Maine. He graduated from North Yarmouth Academy in 1957.

The author received his B.A. degree in education from Eastern Baptist College of St. Davids, Pennsylvania, in 1961, also serving as student council president. He received an M.A. degree in history with Phi Kappa Phi honors at the University of Maine in Orono in 1968. He has always had a particular interest in movements of social and political dissent. He has been an American Studies Fellow with the Coe Foundation, making a study of communal experiments in America. As an N.D.E.A. Fellow at Dartmouth College, he made a study of Toryism in the American Revolution.

His master's thesis was a study of political behavior patterns of the town of his maternal ancestors. It was expanded into a town history and published in 1969 under the title, *History of Parkman*. As a resident of Lee, Maine, he also prepared a twenty-five-town regional study of his own area for high school students of his history classes. It was published in 1971 under the title, *A History of Three Corners*. Both books were purchased in quantity by acts of the Maine legislature for distribution to public libraries around the state.

Storms has taught local history in adult education as well as on the secondary level. In addition to these books, he has written a dozen articles of a historical nature appearing in four periodicals, as well as numerous editorial pieces.

Active in several historical groups, he is on the board of directors of the Lee Historical Society and Museum. An incorporator of the Maine Old Cemetery Association, he served on its board of directors from its founding to the present. Besides his historical lectures, Storms is a licensed lay preacher with the United Baptist Convention of Maine. He is moderator of his local church, and has held various minor offices on local, association, and state level in his denomination. He has also served as interim pastor of the Congregational church in Springfield, Maine.

A fourth generation educator, Storms has taught English, history and government in the schools of Dexter, Greenville, Lee and Lincoln for eleven years. For seven years, he was guidance director and social studies chairman at Lee Academy. He presently teaches history and government at the high school in Lincoln, Maine, while also serving as one of Lee's school board representatives. He has pioneered in several new curriculum changes. His program for teaching religious beliefs in the schools has been the subject of an interview on Maine educational television. He had held several offices in teachers associations including that of local president.

He was married in 1963 to Margaret L. Fry of Kittanning, Pennsylvania. They have two children, a girl age seven and a boy age three. Since 1963, Storms has represented Maine on the Prohibition National Committee. He has served as secretary of the committee since 1969, and a board member of National Prohibition Foundation. He is the founder and national president of the Partisan Prohibition Historical Society.

Roger Storms comes from a family that has held public office in Maine for five generations. One of his great-great-grandfathers was an organizer and winning candidate of the original Maine Law Party of 1854. This book, *Partisan Prophets,* is the product of nearly twelve years of collecting, compiling and writing about this movement.

TABLE OF CONTENTS

CHAPTER I

BEGINNINGS AND BETRAYAL, 1854-1872

There was in 1854 a spontaneous political explosion which created the Republican Party. Its appearance in 1854 has been without parallel in American political history. It was a grass roots outpouring of reform sentiment without any design or direction from the top.

The ostensible reason for the formation of this party was the passage of the Kansas-Nebraska Act which threw open new areas to slavery by repeal of the Missouri Compromise. While the traditional view of the Republican phenomenon has been that this was the sole reason for its formation, this is not an adequate explanation. Such an interpretation ignores decades of growing agitation for broad-based humanitarian reform.

Humanitarian reform was the child of evangelical religious fervor. Fair treatment of labor, equality for women, humane care for the insane and handicapped, prison reform, communitarianism, public education, and world peace were some of the many reforms trumpeted in fiery camp meetings or carried by circuit-riding preachers into the frontier. Most prominent among the ideas which would transform American society were abolition of slavery and the temperance crusade.

None of these reforms were regarded as a cure-all in themselves. Most humanitarians of these early days had a comprehensive view. They tended to be interested in all these causes. What they wanted was a democratic transformation which would create a society of Christian justice and equality.

In the decades preceding 1854, the reformers found little encouragement in the established political parties. The intensity of humanitarian sentiment grew, while the Democrats and Whigs continued to sit on the lid doing nothing. By 1854, the lid was ready to blow off.

The spontaneous nature of the explosion meant that the Republican name was not universally used. The fact that so many names were used points up the comprehensive nature of the movement. Abolition of slavery was not the only issue. Of the other issues linked with slavery, prohibitory laws against the liquor traffic were most often mentioned.

The founders of the Prohibition Party were nurtured in the humanitarian agitation of the decades prior to 1854. They were also a part of the formation of the Republican Party. At least three local, spontaneous parties merged into the Republican movement of 1854, which were direct ancestors of the Prohibition Party through their leaders: (1) Neal Dow's Temperance and Maine Law parties in Maine, (2) Gerrit Smith's Anti-Dramshop Party in New York, (3) and James Black's Prohibition Party of Lancaster County, Pennsylvania. Dow, Smith and Black were all prominent in the formative years of the national Prohibition Party. Their organizations were by no means the only such prohibitory parties, however. There were Temperance parties in Indiana, Ohio, Connecticut and Georgia.

Neal Dow was born in Portland, Maine, of Quaker parents. He entered his father's tanning business and eventually became prominent in several Portland enterprises. Like many who became wealthy, he felt that this obligated him to enter a life of public service. His first office was Overseer of the Poor. In this capacity, he began to see that the liquor traffic was a major cause of poverty.

One day a woman, who was a regular recipient of relief, came to him with a plea. She said that she would be able to support her family if Dow could persuade a particular saloon-keeper to stop serving her husband. He was drinking up his weekly wages at the saloon. When Neal Dow asked the saloon-keeper to stop serving this particular man, he was informed that the liquor-seller had a legal right to sell to whomever he pleased and that he fully intended to continue selling to this particular customer. Neal Dow began to turn this over in his mind, and he began to wonder if the liquor traffic should have the legal right to do as it pleased.

James Appleton had pushed through a temperance law some years before. He had been a general in the War of 1812, a legislator, and abolitionist candidate for governor in Maine three times. Neither he nor Dow advocated a law which would totally ban liquor consumption. Rather, they sought to restrict its excessive use only.

Dow organized the Maine Temperance Union, one of the earliest organizations of its kind. He began to campaign for a prohibitory law, later known as the Maine Law. He was elected mayor of Portland in 1851 and again in 1855. The chief issue in each campaign was prohibition. Using his office of mayor as a springboard, Neal Dow was able to pressure the legislature into enacting the Maine Law. In fact, he himself served in the legislature for two terms.

The idea electrified the reform elements across the country and similar laws were quickly enacted elsewhere. The United Kingdom Alliance even prevailed on Neal Dow to go to the British Isles on three extensive lecture tours for prohibition. However, the established parties sabotaged the prohibitory laws. In few places other than Maine did such laws survive the Civil War in this preliminary outpouring of prohibition sentiment. The utter intransigence of the liquor traffic toward these moderate attempts did, however push temperance leaders toward more inflexible positions.

The reason for prohibitory success in Maine in contrast to elsewhere was the formation of the Maine Law Party in 1853. The two key issues stressed were defense of the Maine Law and opposition to the Kansas-Nebraska Act. The party was an immediate success at the polls and replaced the old Whig Party as the chief opposition to the Democrats. It soon merged into the larger Republican movement which was sweeping the country.

Neal Dow became an enthusiastic Republican. He supported the Civil War as a crusade against slavery, in spite of the fact that it meant expulsion from his Quaker faith. He rose to the rank of brigadier-general in military service. During Admiral Farragut's drive up the Mississippi River to join Grant at Vickesburg, General Dow was twice wounded at the battle for Port Hudson. While recuperating, he was captured by the enemy. During the eight-month ordeal in Libby Prison and elsewhere, his health was broken and he was exchanged for General Fitzhugh Lee. Neal Dow pioneered in the mechanization of the tannery business. He was chief of Portland's volunteer fire fighters, a land developer on the eastern Maine frontier, and a founder of the Maine Central Railroad.

Another important figure in the early abolition and prohibition efforts was Gerrit Smith. He was connected with the Anti-Dramshop Party in New York, which made its first appearance during the same period as the Maine Law Party. The New York effort was successful in electing Myron H. Clark as governor in fusion with the Whigs. Clark too found his way into the Prohibition Party after the Civil War.

Gerrit Smith was a humanitarian of a most comprehensive nature. He was born in Utica, New York and inherited a fairly large fortune, which he devoted to all sorts of philanthropies and reform causes. He was prominent in the American Peace Society, active in prison reform and woman suffrage campaigns, and even contributed to the movements for Italian unification as well as Greek and Irish independence movements.

Gerrit Smith is best known for his work in abolition of slavery. He attempted to set up a Negro colony in the Adirondacks. He was active in the underground railroad and is remembered for his part in the "Jerry rescue" in Syracuse. Smith was an active candidate for governor in the Liberty Party, as was General Appleton. He was elected to a term in Congress as an independent. He financed the free soilers' campaign to settle Kansas and keep it out of the slave-state column. Particularly, he backed John Brown's activities although he was horrified to find Brown using such violent methods.

A third precursor of the Prohibition Party was James Black. Born in Lewisburg, Pennsylvania, James Black came to a turning point in his life at the age of sixteen. While a mule driver on the Pennsylvania and Union Canal, he was forced to accompany the older men on a drinking spree. The experience so disgusted him that he became a life-long enemy of the liquor traffic. He was an early organizer of the Washingtonian Society and later of the International Order of Good Templars. Black organized the National Publication House of the National Temperance Convention, and he had one of the most complete temperance libraries in existence.

James Black entered law practice in Lancaster County, and was a contemporary of Thaddeus Stevens and James Buchanan there. Black formed the Lancaster County Prohibition Party in 1855. Two men were elected to the Pennsylvania legislature on his ticket.

The three examples above are given to illustrate that many who merged to form the Republican Party regarded it as an instrument of comprehensive Christian reform in keeping with the humanitarian spirit of earlier decades. Men like Neal Dow, Gerrit Smith and James Black were particularly concerned about temperance reform. They were willing to let the temperance question remain in eclipse as long as the problem of slavery needed to be solved. But when the question was solved, they expected prohibition to be the next great crusade of the Republican Party.

There was another group of men who viewed the Republican phenomenon in a very different light. The Eastern business community was not concerned about humanitarianism. Rather, they saw in the Republican Party an instrument through which they could institute an economic transformation.

Using the momentum of the Civil War, these capitalists were able to enact a high protective tariff, create the first really national banking and currency system, subsidize the building of railroads, and other programs favorable to business development. An excise tax was placed on liquor, and businessmen began to defend the liquor traffic because of the taxes it provided to the government.

There was much corruption in the collection of liquor excise taxes. There were other things which began to disturb the reformers too—a spoils system in government employment and widespread mismanagement of veterans' pensions. By 1877, Republican businessmen were even ready to give up their civil rights program for the Negro. In order to keep a Republican in the White House, they agreed to give up the Reconstruction program. In return, southern Democrats supported the new capitalism in Congress.

Temperance crusaders began to feel that the Republican Party was betraying its original spirit and aims. At the same time, they did not approve of the constant exploitation of Civil War bitterness. To them this was a phony technique of waving the "bloody shirt." On the surface, it sharply divided the country between northern Republicanism and southern Democracy, while in actual practice the political leaders of both sections joined hands to prevent humanitarian reform.

Gerrit Smith, in spite of his radical abolitionist sentiments, was one of the signers of Jefferson Davis' bail bond. He urged reconciliation with the South. As Neal Dow later put it, "no more solid South, no more solid North, and no more waving of the bloody shirt." Thus, the Prohibition Party was born because its leaders felt that the Republican Party had betrayed its original humanitarian spirit in favor of business as usual. But at the same time they wanted an end to phony sectionalism which diverted attention from the real issues.

On January 8, 1867, forty friends of Methodist clergyman John Russell met in his home to issue a call for the formation of a Prohibition Party. Editor of the **Peninsular Herald** of Detroit, Rev. John Russell spent the next two years promoting the concept of a new party. He was Presiding Elder of the Methodist Church in Michigan for eight years and chairman of the Methodists' national Committee on Temperance. For twelve years he headed the Good Templars in Michigan and headed the world order for two years as well.

Local parties began to appear. There was always spirited debate at each meeting, however, by those who wanted to work within the two-party system. On December 9, 1868, two hundred delegates met in Bloomington, Illinois, to form a state party organization. Many delegates had come to defeat the idea, but in this case their effort failed. There were a number of other instances around the country where they did not fail.

By January 26, 1869, Michigan organized a party and adopted a platform in Jackson, Michigan. Two months later, a Prohibition ticket was entered in the city elections of Cleveland, Ohio. A state organization was completed at Mansfield, Ohio, on July 4, 1869.

A short-lived Temperance Party was launched in Maine with Nathan G. Hitchborn, a United States marshal, as candidate for governor. Hitchborn polled 4,735 votes in a vigorous campaign. His vote would never be equalled on a statewide basis by the Prohibition Party of later years. Following the election, the Temperance Party named Sidney Perham as their choice for governor. The Republicans concurred and thus absorbed the new party back into their ranks. Perham was elected governor in the next election.

Meanwhile, Rev. John Russell continued his pressure for the formation of a national party. He was backed by resolutions passed by various temperance groups, each implying the need for a new party. He finally induced the Good Templars to issue a call for a national convention during their sessions of May, 1869, at Oswego, New York. Fifty-seven residents of some twenty states signed the call for a convention to meet at Farwell Hall in Chicago on September 1, 1869. Among the signers were the national heads of the Sons of Temperance, Good Templars, and Temple of Honor.

About 500 delegates from nineteen states and the District of Columbia attended the three-day convention at Farwell Hall. For the first time in American history, women were permitted to sit on an equal basis with men at a political convention, a tradition that was continued by the Prohibition Party thereafter.

The convention very nearly rejected the idea of a new party. Many were delegates for the express purpose of defeating the idea. Prominent among the delegates who supported the partisan approach was Gerrit Smith, who addressed the convention. "Our involuntary slaves are set free, but our millions of voluntary slaves still clang their chains. The lot of the literal slave, of him whom others have enslaved, is indeed a hard one; nevertheless it is a paradise compared with the lot of him who has enslaved himself—especially him who has enslaved himself to alcohol." His speech was later published as "Address to the People of the United States", calling for support of the new party.

Smith urged the formation of a party and he was backed strongly by J. H. Orne of Massachusetts, head of the Good Templars. A bare majority voted in favor of the idea. At first, they voted to call the new party the National Temperance Party. However, John Russell fought to get them to reconsider the question. The convention agreed and the name "Prohibition Party" was chosen.

Gerrit Smith returned to New York and revived the old Anti-Dram-shop Party. Myron H. Clark, who had been elected governor in 1854, again became their candidate for governor. In Massachusetts, the Prohibition Party nominated Wendell Phillips for governor and was joined by the Labor Reform Party.

In committting himself to run, Phillips changed a lifelong policy of refusing to run for office or to vote in a political system which he regarded as hopelessly corrupt. Wendell Phillips was a handsome, urbane, wealthy Bostonian, famous as a radical gadfly on the Lyceum circuit and as a persuasive speaker for abolition of slavery. Since the Civil War, he had campaigned for prison reform, woman suffrage, and fairer treatment of Indians. During his campaign for governor, he vigorously attacked the evils of the capitalist system and urged workers to organize unions. In spite of the fact that postmasters around the state refused to deliver his campaign literature and ballots, he polled a surprising 21,946 votes, the first sizable showing of a Prohibition candidate.

The following year, Judge Robert C. Pitman was the Massachusetts candidate for governor. Pitman had sponsored prohibition laws during two terms in the state Senate. Rev. George H. Vibbert was elected to the Massachusetts legislature as a Prohibitionist in that campaign. By this time there were Prohibition candidates for statewide office in six states, not to mention coalition candidates with the Republicans in Minnesota and Maine. In Illinois' heavily Republican Eighth Congressional District, George W. Minier waged such a vigorous campaign that the Democratic candidate was elected. Republicans were learning that they could not dodge the issues.

CHAPTER II

THE LEAN YEARS, 1872-1882

Prohibitionists met in Columbus, Ohio, on February 22, 1872, to hold their first nominating convention. The names of several prominent men were proposed for national office, including Benjamin F. Butler and United States Chief Justice Salmon P. Chase. However, the convention decided to name two of its party founders. James Black of Pennsylvania was nominated for president and John Russell for vice president.

Besides a call for national prohibition by constitutional amendment, the platform called for an end to the spoils system through Civil Service reform, regulation of public utilities, sound currency convertible into gold or silver, and better public education. It attacked business monopolies and subsidies by the government, and it called for fair treatment of labor. The platform endorsed woman suffrage with only twenty-two delegates dissenting. Franchise without regard to race was also called for. Finally, a liberal immigration policy was endorsed. All of the above ideas would find wide acceptance in the decades to come. But in 1872, they were ahead of the times.

The new national chairman, Simeon B. Chase, had served many terms in the Pennsylvania legislature as a Republican, including one term as Speaker of the House. Very little campaigning was done in 1872. Most of what was done was through literature distribution. John Russell's **Peninsular Herald** had 5,000 subscribers. A hundred thousand copies of Russell's pamphlet, "An Adequate Remedy for a National Evil," were distributed. Seven college presidents were won to the party, but there were few votes on election day. Six states reported a total of 5,605 for Black and Russell.

Connecticut Prohibitionists nominated a former United States Senator, Francis Gillette, as their candidate for governor in 1872. Gillette ran well ahead of the national ticket and held the balance of power between the two major parties. By 1874, the Prohibition vote in Connecticut had reached five per cent (4,960).

That same year, a humble beginning was made in California, which would one day be the largest arm of the Prohibition Party. The Temperance Reform Party formed in 1874 did no more than call for liquor licenses. The platform also called for government regulation of the railroads, the eight-hour working day, economy in government, and the mingling of physical work with regular book learning. The party's chief newspaper was the **California Voice**, still America's oldest temperance periodical.

In 1875, Rhode Island Prohibitionists polled 8,724 votes for governor, thus throwing the election into the state legislature. Since the candidate was also the Independent nominee, he received a plurality. However, the legislature did not choose him.

The 1876 national convention met on May 17th in Cleveland, Ohio. The name was changed to Prohibition Reform Party. The platform called for the abolition of polygamy, and the suppression of lotteries and gambling. Sunday observance and free use of the Bible in the schools were endorsed. Compulsory education by constitutional amendment was favored. However, no particular religious group was to be favored over any other in education or any other governmental matters.

The party called for arbitration of international disputes. Cruel practices in prison systems were deplored. The new national banking and currency system was criticized, as was the policy on public land. The platform called for land grants only to actual settlers. Direct election of Senators, the President and Vice President was endorsed. All these new issues were incorporated along with those favored four years before.

As a candidate for president, the convention turned to the distinguished Green Clay Smith. Smith's father had been a top aide to William Henry Harrison at Tippecanoe and The Thames, a Speaker of the Kentiucky House, and a Congressman. His mother was the daughter of General Green Clay who had served in the War of 1812.

Young Green Clay Smith was an officer in the Mexican War. Returning to Kentucky, he became a lawyer and legislator. Although a Democrat, he supported the Union cause. Rising to the rank of major-general in the Union army, he defeated General Forest at Rutherford Creek and was wounded at Lebanon, Tennessee.

While still in the field, he was elected to Congress and served two terms. Needing a Democrat for the Union ticket in 1864, many felt that Smith should be Lincoln's running mate. In preliminary caucusing, he was edged out by Andrew Johnson by one vote.

Leaving Congress, he became territorial governor of Montana at a difficult time. There was widespread corruption among white administrators and the Indians had just won the victory at Little Big Horn. Smith handled both corruption and the Indian danger ably. After his term as governor, he felt a call to leave politics and enter the Baptist ministry. As a clergyman, he ministered to one of the nation's most influential congregations for many years—the Metropolitan Baptist Church in Washington, D.C. He became actively interested in the temperance cause and thus agreed to be the Prohibition presidential candidate.

Smith's running mate was Gideon T. Stewart, a long-time local office-holder in Huron County, Ohio. Stewart owned and edited the **Dubuque Times** during the Civil War, the only Unionist newspaper in Iowa. Returing to Ohio, he was editor of various newspapers, particularly the **Toledo Blade** and the **Toledo Commercial.** He headed the Sons of Temperance and the Good Templars in Ohio.

Prospects for the campaign looked considerably better as more than forty newspapers endorsed the Prohibition candidates. There were also strong state candidates such as Dr. Joseph Cummings, president of Wesleyan University, who was candidate for governor in Connecticut. In Massachusetts, there was a strong fusion campaign with the Greenbackers.

But the election provided the first evidences of what would be a long history of voting fraud against the Prohibition Party. In spite of an active campaign in New York, not a single Prohibition vote was reported in Buffalo, Albany or New York City. This was in spite of the fact that several party leaders lived in these cities and rallies had been held there. The vote for Smith and Stewart totaled 9,737 from ten states. Of course, the vote for state tickets continued to be many times more than this. The vote in the ten states for state offices totaled 26,014 in 1876. In off-year elections, the showings were even better. For instance, the vote in six states one year later was 43,230. Several candidates for local offices were elected.

In Rhode Island, General Charles A. Van Zandt, former president of the state Senate, was nominated for governor by the Prohibitionists. The

Republicans agreed to join a fusion and Van Zandt was elected for three successive years.

There were 142 delegates from twelve states at the June 17, 1880, national convention, meeting in Cleveland, Ohio. This time, "Narrow Gauge" Prohibitionists prevailed and the platform spoke almost exclusively on the liquor question. The only other issue endorsed was woman suffrage.

Their choice for president was Neal Dow, who was nominated "by a unanimous rising vote with cheer upon cheer and the doxology." His vice presidential partner was Dr. Henry A. Thompson, who had been a professor of mathematics at various colleges. At the time of his nomination, he was president of Otterbein University. He had also been superintendent of schools in Troy, Ohio, editor-in-chief of Sunday school materials for the United Brethern Church, as well as editor of the **United Brethren Quarterly Review.** Dr. Thompson was the author of five books.

Neal Dow did no active campaigning. Like Gerrit Smith who had returned to the Republicans in 1872, General Dow vacillated on whether to make a complete break with party which had been founded on humanitarian reform. Dow and Smith, along with many others, kept hoping that the Republican Party could be persuaded to return to its original ideals. Privately, he wrote to his friend, James G. Blaine, "I was never a more stalwart Republican than I am now, and so most earnestly wish success to Gen. Garfield."

Blaine released the statement to the press and it was widely circulated. Dow repudiated the remarks and voted for his own ticket rather than Garfield's. But he was glad when Garfield won, and he supported Blaine four years later. However, as time passed, he saw one betrayal after another. By 1885, he declared, "They have spit in our faces and kicked us out. I, for one, am out." Never again did Neal Dow worry about splitting the Republican vote. He spent the rest of his life campaigning tirelessly for the Prohibition Party—far more actively than he had for his own candidacy. Once more he ran for mayor of his native city and was given a large vote on the Prohibition ticket alone.

The damage for 1880 had been done. The vote for Dow and Thompson was only 10,304. Nevertheless, the candidate for governor in Michigan the following year polled 7.7% of the vote and other states reported good showings.

Although the party's following had remained small in these early years, it had attracted a number of distinguished supporters. One of these was Dr. A. A. Miner, a prominent Universalist clergyman. After several years in educational administration on the secondary level, Dr. Miner was called upon to be president of Tufts College. Tufts was in deep financial difficulty. Dr. Miner was able to reorganize and expand the college, while putting it on a sound financial footing. He served as president for twelve years. Thereafter, he promoted Dean Academy in Massachusetts and Goddard Seminary in Vermont. All the while, he was prominent in party strategy sessions behind the scenes. He served as president of Boston's Anti-Tenement-House League. Professor John Bascom was yet another college administrator recruited in these early years. He was president of the University of Wisconsin during thirteen of its most formative years, as well as being important in the party's inner councils. As a scholar, he pioneered in the field of psychology.

Another important adherent was John Sobieski. He was author of a biography about his famous ancestor, King John Sobieski of Poland, who turned back Moslem invaders at Vienna in the seventeenth century. Being the direct descendant of this famous king, young John's father became the central figure in a nationalist uprising against the Russians in 1846. When John was four, his father was executed and his mother was forced to flee to England. At the age of twelve, his mother died and left him alone in a strange land. He came to America and served as an army bugler in the Indian service in the West. During the Civil War, he served as a colonel in the Army of the Potomac. Afterwards, he joined the effort to drive Maximilian out of Mexico. As chief of staff to General Escobedo, he was present at Maximilian's execution.

John Sobieski settled in Minnesota and began the practice of law. As a member of the state legislature, he wrote the first woman suffrage bill to be introduced in the country. He became an active party campaigner for various offices, living well into the twentieth century.

Dr. and Mrs. A. J. Gordon were prominent at many party functions during the period. Dr. Gordon was the author of many books and a leading Baptist clergyman. He edited a monthly magazine, **The Watchword**, and wrote a good deal in behalf of the party as well. A musician, he wrote the tunes for such hymns as "My Jesus, I Love Thee." He also is well known as the founder of Gordon College.

The most striking characteristic of the Prohibition Party was the place occupied by women in the high councils of the party. There are many women like Mrs. A. J. Gordon who could be mentioned. Perhaps the most prominent among them was Mrs. Eliza D. Stewart, popularly known as "Mother" Stewart. She gained her title for her charitable work among the soldiers during the Civil War.

Mother Stewart was on the first national board of charities. She was president of the first local woman suffrage organization. She became known for her eloquent presentations in court suits by drunkards' wives against saloon keepers. She formed a Woman's League in Osborn, Ohio, in December of 1873. This became the first local WCTU, and later she formed the first state WCTU, with Ohio leading the way in this organization. Mother Stewart travelled all over the country organizing for the WCTU. She was particularly active in recruiting Negro women in the South. She joined the Prohibition Party in 1874. Thus, the WCTU was first organized as the women's arm of the partisan effort.

CHAPTER III

REORGANIZATION, 1882-1884

A group of dissatisfied party members met in a summer cottage near Chicago in August of 1881. The meeting has been referred to as the Lake Bluff Convocation. Joining with the group was a dynamic young woman who would dramatically change the course of the Prohibition Party and the WCTU. She was the new president of the National WCTU, Frances E. Willard.

Miss Willard, known to her friends as "Frank," much preferred hunting and horseback riding to housework. Influenced by the writings of Charlotte Bronte and Margaret Fuller, she became a passionate advocate of equal rights for women. But she was not an eccentric like many suffragettes. Her genteel, yet powerful, personality won many thousands of men who were alienated by suffragettes who tried to act like men. Because of this, she became the most important figure in the path toward equal rights for women.

Frances Willard graduated from Northwestern Female College. She taught in two colleges before returning to become president of Evanston College for Ladies. She was closely associated with Terence V. Powderly in developing the Knights of Labor as the earliest national labor organization. She was president of the National Council of Women, and was one of the original founders of what became the Federation of Women's Clubs. But of course, she is best known as president of the National WCTU and the World WCTU. A statue stands in the Capitol's Statuary Hall as one of the two representing the state of Illinois. She was the first woman to be so honored.

Miss Willard did not like the name of the Prohibition Party, and she was supported by certain men in the party who felt that it had not grown fast enough. At the Lake Bluff Convocation, this group agreed to form a new party called the Home Protection Party.

The Prohibition Party leaders responded by agreeing to a joint convention at Farwell Hall, Chicago on August 23 and 24, 1882. Twenty-two states were represented by 341 delegates. Except for the Iowa delegation, the convention agreed to join the two parties under the new name, Prohibition Home Protection Party.

The reorganized party enjoyed the full energy and campaign skills of Frances Willard for the rest of her life. The party also enjoyed the full endorsement and co-operation of the WCTU until she had passed from the scene.

Largely through her efforts, several important new leaders were recruited into the party, for she campaigned in every state and territory of the United States. John B. Gough, an English immigrant, was one. Gough was already famous for his lectures as a reformed drunkard for the Washingtonian Society. Another was Mary T. Lathrap, one of the earliest women to be licensed as a preacher in the Methodist Church. Mrs. Lathrap was a long-time president of the Michigan WCTU and wrote many poems and short articles. She campaigned for the party all over the country.

Of major importance to the development of party propaganda was the recruiting of some key publishers in New York City. Two of these were William Jennings Demorest and his wife, Mary Ellen, known to most as Nell Demorest. Nell invented the original idea of the paper pattern for helping women make their own dresses. Her husband opened a business on Broadway and later on Madison Avenue, where he pioneered in the fashion industry. He kept scouts in Europe to keep him informed on the latest styles, and he set up 1,500 agencies which were soon outselling European firms both at home and in Europe itself.

In order to encourage a large mail-order business, they launched **Mme. Demorest's Mirror of Fashions,** later changed to **Demorest's Family Magazine.** In this magazine, they pioneered in color plates for illustrations, and made Paris fashions available to women on the frontier. They also pioneered in periodicals for the young, with the **Juvenile Bulletin of Fashions** and **Young America** for the children. Much writing on behalf of the temperance crusade appeared in these magazines. In addition, Demorest launched his famous Medal Contests for prohibition essays. He distributed some 42,000 silver, gold and diamond medals to contestants all over the world. About 250,000 declamations were delivered in these contests.

Nell Demorest was a close associate of Frances Willard in her many activities. Nell gave a part of her fortune to the idea that women could own and operate their own businesses. A clipper ship, "Madame Demorest," was launched, the first to be owned and managed by women. She had a key part in the promotion of Mandarin Tea, a considerable success. It was sold widely and was a product developed by Madame Demorest and her female partner.

Nell was an active philanthropist who played a key role in New York City's House of Mercy for Fallen Women, in the New York Medical College for Women, and in a Normal School for Negroes. Meanwhile, her husband distinguished himself as the inventor of the high-wheel bicycle and the hoop skirt. He also invented several improvements on the sewing machine, gas cooking and heating equipment.

William Jennings Demorest was suggested as the Prohibition candidate for governor of New York along with H. Clay Bascom. Bascom, another recruit to the reorganized party, owned the Troy Pattern Works, largest manufacturer of stove patterns in the country. Demorest bowed to Bascom and ran for lieutenant governor. In that campaign and in a campaign for mayor of New York City, Demorest was a vigorous campaigner and a record vote-getter.

Another publisher of major importance who joined the movement was Dr. Issac K. Funk. Funk first came to New York to edit the **Metropolitan Pulpit.** The purpose of the publication was to supply Bible studies and sermon materials for ministers. Its name was changed several times until Dr. Funk settled on the name, **Homiletic Review.** From this he branched out into all sorts of books, illustrations and supplies for clergymen.

With an old classmate, he formed the Funk and Wagnalls Company, which became successful in the publication of standard reference works. Some of their successes were the seventy-nine-volume **Standard Series,** Charles H. Spurgeon's seven-volume **The Treasury of David, The Jewish Encyclopedia** of twelve volumes, and the famous **A Standard Dictionary of the English Language.** The last was particularly the personal work of Dr. Funk.

Dr. Funk developed two periodicals which were of particular significance. First, he founded and edited the **Literary Digest** which grew in prestige over the decades. Second, he launched the **Voice,** which for many years was the chief organ of the Prohibition Party. By the campaign of 1888, this newspaper had a circulation of 700,000.

With party reorganization in 1882 and the conversion of so many distinguished leaders, the results were felt immediately. That fall saw a vote of 25,783 cast in New York and a national total for state tickets of 91,896. In California, Dr. R. H. McDonald, president of the Pacific Bank of San Francisco, made the first good showing there in the race for governor.

The Republicans did nothing to slow down the momentum of the party. They committed a series of blunders which only hastened the growth of the Prohibition Party. Their national standard-bearers of 1884, Blaine and Logan, presented ideas on the distribution of liquor tax revenues for state educational purposes. This did nothing to please the temperance forces.

The WCTU sent Frances Willard to the Republican Platform Committee to plead for a clearer stand on prohibition. She was given a brief hearing and a cold reception. Later, the copy of the WCTU Memorandum which she had presented to them was found on the floor with tobacco juice spit upon it. This was photographed and widely circulated in the temperance press.

Then there was Dr. Richard Burchard's famous boomerang when he referred to the Democrats as the party of "Rum, Romanism and Rebellion." John B. Finch, handsome young chairman of the Prohibition Party and national head of the Good Templars, was present at the Burchard reception given on behalf of the Blaine candidacy. When he heard these words, he jotted them down on a piece of paper. A leading Democrat (Daniel Manning) was standing behind him. Manning snatched the paper from Finch's hand and rushed to the telegraph office. Thus were many Roman Catholic voters alienated from the Blaine campaign.

However, the incident which electrified the Prohibition campaign was concerned with the successful campaign to add a prohibition amendment to the Maine constitution. Maine state elections were held in September before the national election in November. As James G. Blaine came in to vote at his home state precinct, he refused to take the ballot which contained the question of constitutional prohibition. He reasoned that this was a state question with which he should not be involved as a national candidate. News of his decision spread across the country like wildfire.

All of these incidents combined to alienate many from the Republican Party. The Prohibitionists were major beneficiaries. When John P. St. John heard of the treatment given Frances Willard at the Republican convention, he said, "I will condemn such cowardice, such disregard of the best interests of the people with my voice and vote." His conversion to the Prohibition Party was the turning point in the 1884 campaign.

John P. St. John was born in Brooksville, Indiana. His father was an alcoholic and he was left to support himself from the age of twelve. He also entered an unfortunate teenage marriage which ended in divorce. Joining the California gold rush, he had to work at many things to survive. As a sailor, he voyaged to Hawaii, Central and South America. As an Indian fighter, he was wounded twice.

Returning to Illinois, he entered the practice of law. When the Civil War broke out, he became the colonel of an Illinois regiment. After the war, he settled in Kansas and entered the state Senate. Here St. John gained a reputation as a strong opponent of the liquor traffic. The Prohibitionists urged him to be their candidate for governor. But he continued to hope that the Republicans would stand courageously for the "dry" cause.

St. John finally did agree to run under the Prohibition banner if the Republicans would not adopt his idea of prohibition by constitutional amendment. In 1878, however, the Republicans not only endorsed his idea but nominated him for governor as well. He was elected to that office in 1878 and again in 1880. Under the administration of Governor St. John, Kansas became the first state to adopt prohibition by constitutional amendment. Maine followed suit and it was this issue which was the downfall of Blaine as noted above.

Governor St. John was nominated for a third term in 1882. However, the "wets" within his own party worked hard to defeat him and they were successful. Still, he continued to hope up to 1884 that his party would remain the champion of the "drys." The series of events noted above convinced him otherwise. The final break came when Republicans in his own state refused to take a strong stand for prohibition enforcement.

St. John began to tour the country speaking for his cause, and for the first time, states all over the country organized Prohibition Parties. Particularly notable was the formation of the party in Indiana. All the major temperance forces united behind Eli F. Ritter in this effort. Colonel Ritter was a Civil War hero who had fought in most of the major battles on the Tennessee front.

Eli Ritter was a party Prohibitionist of major importance because he established the legal basis for prohibition through the courts. As a skillful lawyer, he won reversal in federal courts of a state supreme court decision in the case, Haggart vs. Stehlin. The case involved saloons in residential areas. The fundamental constitutional question concerned the extent to which liquor licenses entitled saloon keepers to the same civil rights as ordinary, legitimate businesses. The federal courts ruled that the liquor traffic did not come under the category of normal businesses because of the great harm done to the moral tone of the community.

Eli Ritter set a milestone which continued to be the pattern in the courts down to the present day. Later, he was active in prosecuting cases of voting fraud against the political bosses of Indiana. He played a major role in the development of the Prohibition Party in Indiana from 1884 on.

With the gathering momentum on the state level and growing anger with the Republicans, Prohibitionists gathered in Pittsburgh for their convention. Originally scheduled for May, the convention was postponed until July 23 and 24. Many members still hoped for a reconciliation and so they waited until after the major party conventions.

By July, it was clear that neither major party intended to give any quarter. Over seven hundred delegates and alternates came to Lafayette Hall from thirty-one states and territories. The sessions were wildly enthusiastic.

John P. St. John was nominated unanimously for president. The enthusiasm was so great during the nominating speeches, that one seven-minute seconding speech took twenty-seven minutes to deliver. Then after Miss Willard delivered her seconding speech, "every one in the hall arose at one time and hundreds of throats made the air quiver with such loud and prolonged applause that it seemed as if it would never cease."

For vice president, the convention turned to William Daniel, again unanimously. Daniel had delivered the keynote address, interrupted seventy times by applause and demonstrations. He had served two terms in the lower house of the Maryland legislature and one term in the upper house. He was the founding president of the Maryland State Temperance Alliance.

The platform favored the same comprehensive reforms which had been advocated in earlier years. New ones were added supporting the protective tariff and the concept of veterans' pensions. The WCTU received special praise and state parties were urged to work for woman suffrage. But in spite of the mention of other issues, the chief emphasis of the platform was that the liquor traffic was the overriding evil facing the country.

During the campaign, William Daniel campaigned in eight Southern states, besides a tour of New England, Illinois and Wisconsin. St. John was already scheduled to speak in thirty New York camp meetings. Thereafter, he held twenty-eight meetings from Chicago to Massachusetts, eleven of these also in New York. In six major cities, large auditoriums overflowed.

The campaign was strengthened by distinguished men on the state tickets. Among the candidates for governor were: Julius H. Seelye in Massachusetts, president of Amherst College; James B. Hobbs in Illinois, former president of the Chicago Board of Trade; Samuel D. Hastings in Wisconsin, state Treasurer for four terms; and David Preston in Michigan, a leading Detroit banker.

Republicans became alarmed. Top managers for Blaine offered Colonel St. John a bribe to withdraw. When this failed, he was accused of offering to make a deal. Temperance leaders were urged to call for his withdrawal, but few could be found who were not already in the campaign. Personal attacks on St. John were considerable, but it was nothing like what it would be for years after the votes were counted.

St. John's strategy was to capture the state of New York and throw the election into the House or else give the Prohibitionists a balance of power. He failed to carry New York in spite of the vigorous campaign and good leaders. But he was correct that New York held the balance of power. St. John polled 25,016 votes in New York, while Blaine lost the state by 1,047. Had Blaine carried New York, he would have won. Prohibition votes in New York, Connecticut and New Jersey threw the electoral votes for those states to the Democrats.

The total vote for St. John was 153,128, fifteen times the presidential vote four years before. In nearly one hundred communities across the country, St. John was burned or hanged in effigy. Attacks on Prohibitionists were intensified, as ministers were expelled from their pulpits and businessmen were boycotted. The name of St. John County in Kansas was changed to Logan, in honor of Blaine's running mate who was also a Kansan. During the debate, one legislator prayed that St. John's name "be obliterated from Kansas history."

CHAPTER IV

IN THE LIMELIGHT, 1884-1896

In 1885, a National Prohibition Bureau was formed to promote the work of the party. Special emphasis was placed on organization in the South. Over the next two years, the Bureau sponsored 10,000 speeches for the party and distributed ten million pamphlets. Forty different four-page tracts were issued entitled **Prohibition Bombs.** By 1888, its work was merged once again with the National Committee.

The Prohibition candidate for State Treasurer in Kentucky won 27% (29,405) of the vote in 1885, being the only opponent to the Democrats. State tickets in 1886 amassed a vote of 294,863. The party held the balance of power in fourteen states and fifty-eight Congressional districts. Particularly notable was the campaign of Samuel Dickie for governor in Michigan.

Samuel Dickie was destined to have a long and distinguished career. After a brief period as superintendent of schools, he settled down in Albion, Michigan. He served as president of the Albion Buggy Company and was founder and president of the Albion Chamber of Commerce. Later, he was elected mayor of Albion on the Prohibition ticket.

Dr. Dickie was a professor for many years at Albion College. From 1901 to 1921, he was president of the college. At the outbreak of World War I, he was a delegate to the Church Peace Conference in Switzerland. His service to the Prohibition Party began as chairman of the 1884 national convention. After the untimely death of John B. Finch, he served for thirteen years as chairman of the Prohibition National Committee (1887-1900).

Dickie's 1886 campaign for governor in Michigan pushed the party vote over the 25,000 mark. In other states, legislators and office-holders in the major parties were leaving to run for office as Prohibitionists. In Pennsylvania, state legislator Charles S. Wolfe doubled the party's vote for governor (32,458). State Senator E. L. Dohoney ran ahead of the Republicans in fifty-one Texas counties in his race for governor.

In Ohio, the party had the endorsement of twenty-seven newspapers. In Vermont, two Prohibitionists were elected to the legislature, as well as one in Illinois. All over the country, the Republican Party began to make concessions to regain Prohibition votes. However, when they were regained, the concessions were generally repealed or nullified by non-enforcement.

In 1887, two Prohibitionists were elected to the Massachusetts legislature, one of these to the upper house. In New York, there was a rousing state convention at which the majority of the delegates were under the age of thirty-five. The vote in New York reached 41,850.

The national convention of 1888 met at Indianapolis on May 30 and 31. There were 1,029 delegates from forty-two states and territories, not to mention several thousand visitors. There were four hundred from New York alone. The day prior to the convention saw the first national oratorical contest of the Intercollegiate Prohibition Association. This college group, formed by Dr. Herrick Johnson, president of Chicago's McCormick Theological Seminary, became a regular part of the national conventions thereafter.

The gavel of the convention was made from a Kansas telegraph pole on which St. John had been hung in effigy. The objective of 1888 was to make the Prohibition Party a major party. By 1892, they expected a new political alignment in which there would be two parties and a simple choice between "wets" and "drys."

The convention named Clinton B. Fisk as the party nominee for president. Fisk was reared in poverty on the Michigan frontier after his father died at a young age. He was a small banker there until the Panic of 1857. Taking part in the seizure of Camp Jackson, Fisk took a leading part against the Confederate campaigns of Sterling Price in Missouri and Arkansas. He rose to the rank of major-general in the Union cause.

After the Civil War, General Fisk was a leading official of the Freedmen's Bureau in Tennessee. He was in charge of refugees, freed slaves and abandoned lands. When someone objected to his work, President Andrew Johnson made the famous remark, "Fisk ain't a fool, he won't hang everybody." In Nashville, General Fisk began a school for Negroes which became Fisk University.

Thereafter, he became a prosperous New York banker. President Grant appointed him to the Board of Indian Commissioners. He served as president of this board from 1883 until his death. In 1886, he waged a vigorous, four-month campaign for governor of New Jersey in behalf of the Prohibition Party. He made 125 major addresses. Mass meetings were held in every county with many lesser meetings in nearly every town. The party vote was tripled (19,808).

Dr. John A. Brooks was named for vice president. The convention had stresed that sectionalism should end. During the Civil War, Brooks had sympathized with the South while president of a Kentucky college. At the college, he extended hospitality to soldiers of both armies.

The platform was a broad-based one in the scope of reforms which were favored. They called for the abolition of the Internal Revenue system. While accepting the idea of protection of industry, the platform called for reduction of tariffs. Surplus tariff revenues were opposed.

Suffrage on an educational basis only was endorsed. Monopoly and excessive pricing in business were condemned. It called for arbitration of disputes between labor and management. Some immigration restrictions were urged for the first time, but only for criminals or those who were physically and mentally unfit. The franchise for immigrants before obtaining citizenship was opposed. There was also a resolution urging statehood for the Dakotas and condemning the major parties for not approving such status for them.

The only controversy occurred over the question of woman suffrage. The platform also urged "equal wages for equal work" between the sexes. Neal Dow was not favorable to the concept of equality of the sexes. He was joined by a few others and a floor fight developed under the leadership of Rev. Samuel W. Small of Georgia, who saw the issue as harmful to the progress of the party in the South. But when the vote was taken, 95% of the delegates voted for the suffrage plank.

Samuel Small was a "Narrow Gauge" Prohibitionist. Some years before, he had been a well-known columnist for the **Atlanta Constitution** under the pen name of "Old Si." Thereafter he was a court reporter and attaché of the American commission to the Universal Exposition in Paris.

He fell victim to alcoholism until converted. At the 1888 convention, he was a newcomer to the party. By 1894, he led the campaign which elected a Prohibition administration in Norfolk, Virginia. In later years, he was the Anti-Saloon League's most highly paid lecturer.

A half-million copies of the 1888 platform were distributed. Fisk's notification was held in the Metropolitan Opera House in New York, then one of the largest auditoriums in the world. It drew an overflow crowd. Unlike presidential elections before and after 1888, there was no farmer-labor party to offer a comprehensive program of social justice. Fisk appealed directly to these groups in his acceptance.

It is not enough that we reform the individual; we must reform the State. The policy of great commonwealths, of a whole people, must be remade and put in harmony with sound economic principles, the true cooperation of industrial effort, the essential conditions of national prosperity, and the genuine brotherhood of man.

General Fisk had planned a vigorous campaign. However, after a tour of New England, his health would not permit it. Thereafter, he made just a few appearances. One of these was Prohibition Day Celebration in Columbus, Ohio. It took two hours for the parade to pass the reviewing stand. The Coliseum was packed both in the morning and the afternoon to hear the addresses.

A mile-long parade was staged in Poughkeepsie, New York, for the campaign. In Minneapolis, a parade two miles long was led by Hugh Harrison, the city's leading banker and Prohibition candidate for governor.

The National Committee spent $33,397 on the campaign. In addition, the readers of the **Voice** contributed enough money to send the paper to 60,000 clergymen and 500,000 farmers during the campaign. The same Republican official who had sought to bribe St. John four years before, also purchased 50,000 names stolen from the **Voice** mailing list. When the votes were in, General Fisk had not polled the vote expected. However the vote (249,945) was up 70% over the previous election.

The National Committee met in Louisville in 1889 to map further strategy. Plans called for a party organization in every state and territory. Special attention was to be given to winning those of foreign birth. However, only among Scandinavians was this effort particularly successful. Emphasis was also placed on Junior Prohibition Clubs.

In elections of that year, J. B. Helwig, former president of Wittenberg College, was candidate for governor in Ohio. Another helpful campaigner from the college community was Dr. C. H. Payne, president of Ohio Wesleyan University. By 1890, there were Prohibition organizations in all states except Nevada and seven southern states.

The Tennessee state convention drew 416 delegates from fifty-seven counties. In two years of work, eighty-two of ninety-six counties were organized and all but one of the ten Congressional districts. The candidate for governor, Dr. D. C. Kelley, was forced out of his pastorate by the Methodists for his party activities.

The first successful party candidate for Congress was elected in 1890. Kitel Halvorsen, a Minnesota Scandinavian, won with the support of the Farmers' Alliance.

Four thousand delegates and visitors were present on June 30, 1892, for the Cinncinnati national convention. Judge Gresham, an observer there, called it "the most moral and the most intelligent convention that the American people have seen." Prominent among the delegates was Father Mahoney, the party's chief hope of reaching Roman Catholic immigrants. Convention decorations featured white roses, the symbol of the party during this period.

The platform contained more planks on issues other than liquor than any previous platform. There was a lively contest over the plank on currency. The convention defeated a proposal for free and unlimited coinage of silver by a wide margin. However, the platform called for an increase in the volume of money to meet the demands of a growing population. A system of gold, silver and paper money was endorsed, but the volume was to be fixed on a per capita basis. The supply should remain flexible with the population growth.

The second issue which brought a floor fight was the tariff. The convention opposed protective tariffs except as reprisal against barriers of other nations upon our products. By inference, the platform was urging reciprocal trade agreements. Tariffs for revenue purposes were also opposed. The platform urged a tax on income rather than on consumption of goods.

For the first time, the platform called for restriction of immigration which was "depressing wages and causing discontent." Naturalization procedures should be more difficult and new citizens should not vote until a year after naturalization. They also urged that non-resident aliens be prohibited from owning land in this country. Furthermore, railroad land grants should be retracted. In fact, they even favored limitations on the amount of land an individual or corporation could own.

Prohibitionists condemned the major parties for the violence in labor disputes and called for fair treatment of individuals in the courts. They seemed to be condemning by inference the private armies of the industrialists who were taking the law into their own hands. Speculation in grain or money, pooling, trusts and other forms of price-fixing were specifically condemned.

They urged that the government restrict excessive prices by the public utilities. Workingmen should be guaranteed by law one day of rest out of seven. Opposition was expressed to public money for sectarian schools. They advocated a united school system and emphasized that the education be in the English language "to become and remain a homogeneous and harmonious people."

A strong condemnation was delivered against the corruption of city political machines. They defended the secret ballot and condemned widespread election frauds.

Frances Willard was anxious to merge the Prohibition Party with the Populist Party effort. She envisioned one great reform party which would bring about a comprehensively Christian transformation of American society. She appealed to the National Committee to send a delegation to the Populist convention in the hope that they would incorporate prohibition and suffrage planks into their platform. Then the two parties could join behind one candidate.

The Populists were largely a coalition of southern racists and anti-urban westerners. The Prohibition Party centers were in the East and many of its leaders were oriented toward urban life. Miss Willard's proposed merger was opposed by Colonel St. John.

St. John found a powerful ally in Helen Gougar of Indiana. One of the early women to acquire a college education, Mrs. Gougar had graduated from Hillsdale College in 1860. Later, she was the first woman to be elected to the Hillsdale College board of trustees. One of the pioneer women in the field of law, she wrote the Kansas law granting municipal suffrage to women. For fifteen years, she was president of the Indiana Woman Suffrage Association. She travelled widely and became famous for her travel literature on life in foreign lands. She and her husband became wealthy lawyers in Indianapolis.

Helen Gougar and Frances Willard had always been rivals in the various activities which they had in common. On the issue of Populism, Mrs. Gougar joined with Governor St. John in blocking Miss Willard's idea. The National Committee decided not to send a delegation to the Populist convention. Frances Willard and her associates decided to go anyway.

A floor fight developed among the Populists as to whether her delegation should be seated. Her cause was strongly supported by Terence V. Powderly, head of the Knights of Labor, with whom she had been a close associate for many years. Although Frances Willard's delegation was seated, the Populists refused to adopt either prohibition or woman suffrage planks. As it turned out, the Eastern labor movement also received little consideration for their support of Populism.

Miss Willard went to the Prohibition national convention disappointed but still loyal to her old party. She was warmly received by the delegates and hailed by the convention chairman, Eli Ritter, as the first lady of the Prohibition Party. As noted above, the party's platform did assume a strongly Populist tone, in spite of the rejection of an outright free silver plank. It also took on a strongly Western flavor in the nominees it chose, despite the fact that the party's chief base of power was in the East.

For the first time, there was a real contest for the presidential nomination. However, General John Bidwell of California won on the first ballot over three Eastern opponents. John Bidwell was reared in frontier conditions. In order to attend Kingsville Academy in Ashtabula, Ohio, he had to walk 300 miles. The following year, they were sufficiently impressed with his work to make him principal of the school.

Bidwell organized the first group of settlers to cross into California. There were sixty-nine in the party including the Jesuit priest, Father De Smet, pioneer missionary to the Indians in the Northwest. Bidwell was working at Sutter's Mill when gold was discovered, and he played a leading part in the formation of the Bear Flag Republic.

He acquired the 25,000-acre Rancho Chico. Here he developed 1,200 acres of orchard, developed a floor mill, fruit cannery, vinegar works and dairy. He brought more than 200 Indians under his protection, personally administering their education and religious life. He explored most of the streams of the Sacramento Valley and gave them most of the English names they still bear.

During the Civil War, there was strong Southern sympathy in northern California. John Bidwell became a brigadier-general in the state militia, and he played a leading part in the suppression of secessionist activity in the region.

In politics, he served in the state legislature, became one of the earliest advocates of a transcontinental railroad, and took a leading part in founding schools of higher education in California. He served one term in Congress as chairman of the Agriculture Committee. A man of strong Populist views, he polled a quarter of California's votes as the 1875 Anti-Monopoly candidate for governor. Thereafter, he became identified with the Prohibition Party. Already some years before, he had torn up his vineyards after he saw what wine was doing to his fellow man.

For vice president, Dr. James B. Cranfill of Texas was chosen. A frontier doctor, teacher and preacher, he was superintendent of Baptist missionary work on the Texas frontier. He also edited **The Baptist Standard.** A fiery orator, he was the youngest man ever nominated for vice president, being not yet thirty-five.

The party gained little by its Western Populist orientation. Bidwell was prevented from active campaigning by a financial cirsis in California. He was forced to stay at home to save his business. James Cranfill began a tour of the South but was forced out of active campaigning by his health. The party was overshadowed by the Populists in the South and West anyway. It was in the Northeast where reform-minded voters preferred Prohibitionists to Populists. The Prohibition vote ran ahead of the Populists in the East by more than 74,000. The Prohibition presidential vote reached the highest point in its history, both in numbers and in percentage. Bidwell won 271,058 ballots or 2.3% of the national total.

Local election victories began to pile up in the early years of the decade. Several seats were captured in state legislatures: one each in Vermont, Massachusetts (for two terms), Connecticut and Virginia, plus two in Rhode Island. Mayors were elected in New Bedford and Haverhill, Massachusetts; Ogdensburg, New York; Washington, New Jersey; Norfolk, Virginia; Nashville, Tennessee; Williamsport, Pennsylvania; Marinette, Wisconsin; Wellsville, Ohio; and Abion, Michigan. In addition to these, there were several hundred lesser offices won. In some smaller communities, the entire ticket was elected, as it was in seven Colorado towns in 1894. Sometimes even these lesser office-holders found themselves drawing much attention to the party. When a Prohibition candidate for coroner was elected in Gibson County, Indiana, he found himsef in the middle of a celebrated mortality case where liquor was involved.

CHAPTER V

A PRAGMATIC RECONSTRUCTION, 1896-1908

A reaction against the party's drift toward Populism began to harden in 1895 and 1896. Many felt that the party had become too preoccupied with other issues, while the liquor traffic was the paramount problem facing the country. "Narrow Gauge" Prohibitionists wanted all who agreed on that issue to feel comfortable in the party regardless of how they felt on any other question. "Broad Gauge" Prohibitionists countered that voters would not have sufficient faith in a party which spoke on only one issue. They needed to see that the Prohibition Party was prepared to deal with all questions confronting the American people.

Party newspapers were full of the arguments of the two factions for months before the 1896 convention, which assembled in Pittsburgh on the last day of May. The Resolutions Committee reported a broad platform. As each plank was brought up, it was approved by the convention until the plank calling for free silver was presented. This was defeated.

Immediately after its defeat, a motion was presented to substitute a brief, single-issue platform for the one presented by the Resolutions Committee. The motion was carried, 650-160. Free Silver Prohibitionists walked out of the convention. Meeting at another hall, they drafted a platform similar to that of 1892. Free and unlimited coinage of silver on a ratio of sixteen-to-one was also endorsed, plus the income tax, government ownership of public utilities, initiative and referendum. They condemned contract labor and convict labor systems.

The group named their faction the National Party, although they were known as the Liberty Party in Nebraska and were widely referred to as the Free Silver Prohibition Party. For president, they named Charles E. Bentley, a Nebraska Baptist minister who had been the key party leader in that state. For vice president, they turned to a member of the platform committee which the convention had repudiated. James H. Southgate was prominent in North Carolina banking and insurance companies. He was president of the state YMCA and president of the Trinity College board of trustees. Many free silverites among the Prohibitionists, however, simply went on over to join Bryan's Populist-Democratic campaign. The National Party polled only 13,969 votes.

Meantime, the Prohibition Party proceeded to campaign on a platform of unusual brevity, speaking only on the issues of prohibition and woman suffrage. The platform asserted "that we declare our purpose to organize and unite all the friends of prohibition into one party, and in order to accomplish this end we deem it but right to leave every Prohibitionist the freedom of his own convictions upon all other political questions . . ."

For president, the convention chose Joshua Levering as its nominee. Levering was the nation's largest coffee importer outside of New York, centering his business activity in the port city of Baltimore. He was a leading officer in the YMCA and the Baltimore YMCA president for many years. He was also a top officer in the Southern Baptist Convention for a long time, and president of the Southern Baptist Theological Seminary board of trustees.

His vice presidential running mate was Hale Johnson, a lawyer who had led many prohibitory crusades throughout the Midwest. Levering and Johnson both travelled extensively during the campaign. But due to the disheartening effects of the split, the popular vote was cut in half. Levering polled 130,617 votes. Many newspapers announced the impending death of the Prohibition Party.

Three weeks after the election, 170 Prohibitionists met in Poughkeepsie, New York. In twelve minutes, they pledged $12,000 to renew the party and carry on the fight.

Meantime, the structure and nature of the Prohibition Party was changing. The ideological split of 1896 had been a prelude of the change. During the final decade of the nineteenth century, most of the old party leaders had passed away. The old leaders had been prophetic in spirit, declaring what was right regardless of the consequences. They had been reared in the humanitarian-romanticist traditions of the abolitionists and tempered by the fires of the Civil War. By the end of the century, Neal Dow, Frances Willard, Clinton Fisk, John Bidwell, John P. St. John, James Black and many others were gone.

As they passed from the scene, a younger, tougher breed of men replaced them. Many of them, like Samuel Small, were "Narrow Gaugers" and many who held this view were pragmatic in spirit. That is, they did not hold to the old romantic, prophetic belief that the Prohibition Party could be an instrument of comprehensive social change for Christian justice.

There were now those in the party who began to question its Christian emphasis. The party had always stressed its evangelical foundations. But in 1902, there was a vigorous debate at the Iowa state convention. Many delegates present wanted to disassociate the party from outright religious affirmations in order to bring Deists, Jews and other groups into the organization. While this view did not prevail in Iowa, the debate it illicited was widely publicized.

The pragmatic leaders of the new generation wanted to portray prohibition as a simplistic cure-all, which would make all other problems melt away once it was accomplished. As such, they regarded the Prohibition Party as an instrument of a single issue. The new generation was not as willing to stick by a party, "win or lose," in the old prophetic fashion. They were interested in success and they were often willing to use opportunistic methods. Once their single objective was achieved, they would leave the party in droves. They did not understand that their country could never have prohibition or any other Christian reform without a party with Christian views and Christian men. The Prohibition Party survived through the work of the few who understood this and carried on when the pragmatists had returned to the major parties.

John B. Finch, in the last speech before he died, spoke the great, uncompromising truths of a partisan prophet.

> Today, if I could pass a Prohibition law in the State of Massachusetts and I could not put officers in power in sympathy with it, I would not pass the law, because people would say that the law is a failure, when the failure would not be due to the law but to the perjured rascals who swore to enforce the law and did not. The naked sword of justice in the hands of a determined party is the only instrument that will bring the desired results . . .

There were many among the pragmatic new leaders who could not see that it was better to do without moral reform than to achieve a law which would be made a farce by parties of the old politics. Frances

Willard had coined the phrase "New Politics" to describe what the partisan prophets had been trying to do. Typical of the other view was John G. Woolley.

Woolley began a promising career as a lawyer. He served as city attorney of Paris, Illinois, and was elected prosecuting attorney of Minneapolis. However, his career was ruined by drinking and he became a hopeless alcoholic until converted by some Christian friends. Thereafter, he became active in the Prohibition Party. He became famous as an orator, the most famous in the later prohibition movement. He spoke in every major English-speaking city of the world during his career on the platform.

In 1899, the **Voice** was purchased from Funk and Wagnalls. John Woolley merged it with another paper in Chicago and launched **The New Voice** as its editor. But despite the highest honors which the party could give, he rejoined the major parties at the opportune time. The new nonpartisan Anti-Saloon League was heavily financed by the great financiers whose chief purpose was divorce the temperance movement from other reforms which sought economic justice. Woolley acted as keynote speaker in 1913 at their national convention. In his address, he declared: "The Prohibition Party was like a fire bell. It awoke the people. They are up and doing . In such a case there are two things to do, ring the bell more or put out the fire. I am for putting out the fire, whatever becomes of the bell."

In short, the Prohibition Party was a temporary, pragmatic instrument of pressure on the major parties, to be discarded at the expedient moment. This is not to say that all "Narrow Gaugers" were pragmatists. There have always been many loyalists of that school of thought in the party. Nor were all members of the new generation pragmatic by any means. But many were both "Narrow Gauge" and pragmatic.

The new national chairman of 1900 was only thirty-one years old. The party began to stir under younger leadership. In Indiana, the party was able to maintain a full-time organizer-evangelist in each Congressional district. As their candidate for governor, they recruited a leading industrialist, Charles Eckhart. In Kentucky, John D. White was won to the party, a two-term Congressman. Another convert was L. C. Hughes, former territorial governor of Arizona.

State conventions were also rousing occasions in many states. The Indiana convention drew nearly six hundred delegates that year. The keynote speaker was the president of Taylor University, T. C. Reade. Also prominent on the convention program was Charles M. Fillmore. He and his brother, J. H. Fillmore, were the composers of many hymns which may be seen in any church hymnal today. Both were active in the party. J. H. Fillmore is particularly well-known for "I Am Resolved," "The Beautiful Garden of Prayer," and the chorus, "I Will Sing of the Mercies of the Lord Forever." Besides their many hymns, these brothers wrote many of the stirring songs of the Prohibition Party campaigns. A book of these was published at the turn of the century.

Another poet and song-writer for the cause was William G. Brooks of Saco, Maine. He wrote the song, "The Saloon Has Got to Go" along with many others. He was a poet and musical composer of considerable breadth. He wrote marches which were used all over the country by band leaders like John Philip Sousa. "Governor Burleigh's March" and "Light and Airy" were examples. He wrote comic folk songs like "Barney Will Come Back to Me" and "De Water in de Ribber Might Be Wet." He

88375

College of St. Francis Library
Joliet. Illinois

composed many programs for special church holidays and his hymns appeared in at least fifteen hymnal editions.

The national convention of 1900 met in Chicago. There were 735 delegates from thirty-seven states, besides several thousand visitors. Although the platform was the longest one yet, it dealt with only one issue. The "Narrow Gaugers" were definitely in control.

A particularly strong issue was the army canteen, the selling of liquor at army installations. Although Congress outlawed liquor at army bases lying in dry areas, this had been disregarded by government directives. The Spanish-American War had intensified the issue, for now Prohibitionists felt that the country had a new obligation to set a good example for the people of its new overseas possessions. In fact, the party maintained that excessive drinking had been accelerated by the arrival of Americans in such places as Cuba, Puerto Rico and the Philippines. The issue was raised in that platform in a particularly bitter attack on President McKinley and his cabinet. The platform was also anti-imperialistic in tone.

A spirited contest developed over the presidential nomination. John G. Woolley was opposed by Silas C. Swallow. Dr. Swallow was one of the old-style prophetic Prohibitionists. Puritanical to the extreme, he condemned tobacco, swearing and amusements in a most fiery style. So warm was his support of the Union during the Civil War that his Pennsylvania parishioners padlocked the church doors. He served as editor of the **Pennsylvania Methodist** and was superintendent of their book rooms. Later, he edited the the **Church Forum.**

In 1897, he published an exposé of the notorious Quay Republican machine of Pennsylvania. He was tried for libel and acquitted. The following year he ran for State Treasurer on the Prohibition ticket, calling for honesty in state finances. He polled 118,000 votes and carried eleven counties. Two years later, he garnered 132,931 votes for governor.

"Broad Gaugers" rallied around Swallow and "Narrow Gaugers" backed Woolley. Single-issue men had already prevailed in the platform, but the vote was close. Woolley won over Swallow, 380-320.

The vice presidential choice was Henry B. Metcalf, a famous Rhode Island manufacturer and banker. Metcalf had been president for five years of the national conventions of the Universalist Church. He served as president of the Tufts College board of trustees. Before being forced out of the Republican Party on the issue of prohibitory enforcement, he had served a term in the Rhode Island state Senate.

Woolley opened the campaign with a tour of the Pacific coast. Then he joined Metcalf in a whistlestop campaign by special train. Beginning in the Dakotas and Nebraska, the train route went to Boston, back to Minnesota and southward into Tennessee. The train reached eight to fifteen cities per day beginning on September 19 and continuing until the November elections. Woolley delivered nearly 500 addresses and travelled 23,000 miles. No presidential candidate up to that time had travelled so extensively during a campaign. Woolley even exceeded Bryan's record of four years before.

Woolley and Metcalf polled a vote of 209,469 (1.5%) thus restoring much of the support lost in the split of 1896. Within two months after the election, the party received $25,000 to carry on new campaigns in the following years. Congress also responded to the pressure by outlawing the army canteen once again.

The party was further electrified by events in Maine. Cumberland County was the most populous county in the state. There were over one hundred islands in Casco Bay, which made it a rum-runners' paradise. Two Boston firms paid the Republican sheriff's department a dollar for each barrel of liquor landed. There were 277 holders of federal liquor tax receipts in Portland. Yet the federal government made no effort to cooperate in the enforcement of state laws. Everyone pointed to Cumberland County as a prime example of the unenforceability of prohibition.

Rev. Samuel F. Pearson served the poor of Portland in his Gospel Mission. He saw what the liquor traffic was doing to his people in open defiance of law. Neither major party would cooperate with him to change the situation, so he organized an active Prohibition Party.

By 1900, his campaign began to get strong response. Three-term Republican alderman, Zenas Thompson, and spirited Democratic orator, Dr. E. S. J. McAllister, joined Pearson's fight to be elected sheriff of Cumberland County. An open-air meeting in the city of Westbrook drew so many of the leading citizens that the city board of aldermen was unable to hold its regular sessions for lack of a quorum. A spirited meeting was held in suburban Yarmouth's Masonic Hall. That town was carried by a clear majority over the combined vote of the two major parties. On election eve, a rally was held in Portland City Hall auditorium, one of the largest meeting places at that time. The auditorium was packed with many left standing. When the votes were counted, Pearson had a comfortable plurality. His total was 6,425, more votes than any Prohibitionist had ever polled in Maine, even in statewide contests.

On his first day in office alone, Sheriff Pearson seized sixty-one liquor outlets. The local tax burden had grown considerably and the county was in debt. At the end of Pearson's first year in office, 40% of the pauper fund was turned back to the county, the debt was paid, and there was a surplus in the treasury. Business surveys revealed an increase in spending in all sorts of commodities. Even hotels found business better without liquor. In spite of an attempt to bribe Pearson to the tune of $35,000, nearly everyone agreed that he had dried up the county. Even many drinkers testified that they were better off.

Samuel Pearson died before his term expired and he was succeeded by Almon S. Bisbee of Brunswick. In 1902, the party spearheaded an effort to capture the sheriff's offices across the state. They struck at the very heart of the enforcement problem and sent out a ripple of reform activity across the state even in the major parties. Prohibitionists received unusually great support from the churches of the state to elect their candidates for sheriff.

In Cumberland County, Almon Bisbee waged a vigorous campaign for election in his own right. His campaign had the style and personnel of 1900 all over again. He polled 5,102 votes in 1902, but the Democratic candidate was elected. Elsewhere in such counties as Piscataquis, the party vote for sheriff was also large. In Androscoggin County, the Republican Party joined the Prohibitionists in supporting John L. Cummings, who was elected. In Portland, the Democrats and Prohibitionists joined to elect Oakley C. Curtis to the state legislature. In both races, the contest was close and the Prohibition votes were crucial. Oakley Curtis went on as a Democrat to have a long political career in the legislature, as mayor of Portland, and governor of Maine.

Nor was he the only politican to use the Prohibition Party as a launching pad for greater things. The party's candidate for governor in 1894 was Ira G. Hersey. Soon after the campaigns of 1900 and 1902, Hersey became a Republican legislator and served a term as state Senate president. He went on to be a judge and a Congressman from Maine for ten years. Many of the principal figures of the Maine campaigns regarded the Prohibition Party as a temporary, pragmatic instrument of pressure on the old parties of the old politics.

In 1901, the National Committee started a successful new program of local organization. There were local groups called Prohibition Alliances. When formed, they agreed to meet once a month and their numbers were urged to purchase shares in the party work of five cents per share per month. The money raised was divided among local, state and national organizations. The national office provided materials and programs. Within three years, more than 1,800 Prohibition Alliances were formed throughout the country.

Another organization of the period was the Young People's Prohibition League. While it was chiefly confined to a few cities in New York, New Jersey and Pennsylvania, it enlisted many of the young to the party and held many street meetings. There were various other types of local associations which promoted party work. For instance, there was the Prohibition Union of Christian Men in Rochester, New York. Its leader, Clinton N. Howard, delivered 1,200 addresses for the cause in Rochester over a twenty-five-year period.

The Intercollegiate Prohibition Association nearly fell apart after the split in 1896. But at the turn of the century, the National Committee encouraged its revitalization. Known on local college campuses as Prohibition Leagues, the Intercollegiate Prohibition Association was a training ground for most of the party's new leaders. At its height, there were Prohibiion Leagues on nearly 400 campuses and it was the nation's second largest organization of college students, exceeded in size only by the college department of the YMCA and YWCA.

The Association pushed for courses in alcoholic studies, and by 1916 there were more than one hundred colleges which had made such courses a regular part of their curriculums. In addition, it maintained the nation's most extensive system of oratorical contests. The organization supplied many of the party's volunteer workers during summer vacations. In 1901, twenty-four students devoted the summer to the Ohio campaign alone. The chief officers of the Intercollegiate Prohibition Association were always party members. However, in pragmatic fashion, much of its energies were devoted to non-partisan prohibitory crusades. By 1919, it was organizing chapters in European universities.

The 1904 national convention gathered at Indianapolis. This time, the "Broad Gaugers" were in command. Silas C. Swallow was nominated for president by acclamation. His vice presidential partner was George W. Carroll.

George Carroll owned extensive timber lands around Beaumont, Texas. He was prominent in the operation of rice mills. As president of the Yellow Pine Oil Company, he pioneered in drilling for oil and saw it become a major Texas industry. He was a philanthropist, particularly to Baylor University, and had been elected as an alderman of Beaumont.

Among the issues endorsed by the platform were initiative and referendum, an omni-partisan tariff commission, popular election of United

States Senators, and others previously advocated in the older platforms. Dr. Swallow campaigned actively around the country. His vote nearly equalled the record of 1892. Swallow and Carroll polled 258,205 votes. Their campaign buttons had proclaimed that the "Swallows will sing Carrolls."

The period saw a revival in local victories as well. In Venango County, Pennsylvania, a new method called the Venango Plan began to bear fruit. Th Venango Plan urged the voter to sign a pledge to vote for any Prohibition candidate who got a majority of voters to make such a pledge. If a majority of the voters would not make such a pledge, then those who had signed were released from it. It was pragmatic in nature for the emphasis was placed on voting Prohibition only if they could win. The older prophetic generation had stressed voting for the Prohibition Party on principle regardless of any prospects for victory or defeat.

A system similar to the Venango Plan was first used with success in the Pearson campaign of 1900. In 1901, a sheriff was elected in Venango County by this method along with several local officials. In 1904, there were 205 local officials elected in Venango County, and 167 in thirteen other counties the following February. In 1905, the Venango Plan was used in Oswego County, New York, and forty-two Prohibitionists were elected.

In Illinois, there were legislative gains. National chairman, Oliver W. Stewart, won a seat from the Hyde Park district of Chicago in 1902. When the legislature was receiving party nominations for United States Senator, he drew widespread attention by delivering a passionate speech to a packed gallery for John G. Woolley as the Prohibition nominee. In 1904 and 1906, there were three Prohibitionists elected to the Illinois legislature. One of those elected in 1904 represented the city of Peoria. Another was re-elected and served two terms during these years.

The Illinois party organization was greatly aided when it formed the Lincoln Temperance Chautauqua System. Each summer, a series of six-day meetings were held with two meetings per day. A variety of speakers and entertainment was provided. It served a double purpose of building the party and helping non-partisan local option campaigns. It was successful in both respects. Over one hundred communities were reached each season for several years. Eventually, the idea was taken over by non-partisan groups and done on a national scale.

The 1906 elections saw one Prohibitionist legislator elected in each of five states: West Virginia, Massachusetts, Pennsylvania, Connecticut and Florida. Some of these also had support from other minor parties or independent groups. Of course, there were many other legislators elected with the nomination of the Prohibition Party and the nomination of a major party.

The Illinois candidate for State Treasurer carried five counties and ran second in several others in 1906. The party continued to attract distinguished people into its state organizations. In Georgia, Walter B. Hill, president of the Georgia Bar Association and chancellor of the University of Georgia, was won to the party.

The most notable victories of the period came in Minnesota, for it was there that the party was able to sustain its power over a longer period. Beginning in 1904, college men of the Intercollegiate Prohibition Association went to work to elect legislators. In that first try there were no victories. However, there was a large party vote and two hair-thin misses. In 1906, thirty-two college men worked in the field and the vote rose to

32,000. There were three victories, plus a sheriff elected in Kandiyohi County.

Fifty college men worked on the 1908 campaign and the legislative vote rose to 53,000. Three men were elected to the legislature again and the sheriff was re-elected. In addition, Miss Marie Lovsness was elected county superintendent of schools and other local office-seekers won. In 1910, there were five legislative victories including one Senate seat. The sheriff won a third term and Miss Lovsness was also re-elected. By 1914, the number of legislators had risen to seven.

The crowning example of opportunism in a pragmatic age came when John G. Woolley left the party and **The New Voice** collapsed. A new paper was launched as the chief party organ in 1907, **The National Prohibitionist.** The paper enjoyed a circulation of about 200,000. A Chicago lawyer for a whiskey trust concocted a libel suit against the editor of the new paper. Then he ordered the legal machinery of Cook County to prosecute the case. So flimsey was the evidence that the jury took less than five minutes to return an acquittal. Later, the same lawyer for the whiskey trust played a leading part in securing Warren G. Harding's nomination for the presidency.

CHAPTER VI

THE PLATEAU OF PRESSURE POLITICS, 1908-1920

Columbus, Ohio, was the site of the 1908 convention. There were 1,126 delegates. Among them was Carry A. Nation, whose "hatchetation" had already made her live up to her name. Also present was the dogged campaigner of Great Britain's Prohibition Party, Mr. Scrymgeour. In 1922, he became the only man to defeat the anti-prohibition Winston Churchill in the "wet" city of Dundee, Scotland. Scrymgeour was the only partisan Prohibitionist so elected in Britain.

It was decided to publish a platform which would be brief enough to print on a post card and to encourage people to read it. Although it contained but 321 words, it was comprehensive in nature. Besides the older issues, the platform called for graduated income and inheritance taxes, postal savings banks, federal insurance of bank deposits, stricter laws on prostitution, uniform marriage and divorce laws, employer liability laws, court review of Post Office Department decisions, prohibition of child labor, English literacy tests for voting, conservation of natural resources, and construction of better highways and waterways.

A choir of 150 voices, directed by hymnologist Charles M. Fillmore, was one of the musical features of the convention. Walter Wellman, famous Arctic explorer turned reporter, covered the convention. He made a report which is now often used in praise of the calibre of the men who led the party. The convention was "impressive in its love for humanity," and the delegates were "the only purely unselfish actors in the national political arena." There were "no spoils of office to give them zeal." Yet, he confessed, "One cannot help liking these old-fashioned people, these people fighting for principle."

There were nine candidates for the presidential nomination. The heavy favorite up to the time of balloting was William P. Palmore of Missouri. An officer in the Confederate army during the Civil War, he had become a prominent Methodist clergyman. He was editor of the **St. Louis Christian Advocate** and prominent in several world ecumenical conferences. Interested in mission work, he had travelled all over the world, taking a leading part in the formation of Collegio Palmore in Mexico and Palmore Institute in Japan. He was president of the board of curators for Central College for Women. Palmore founded a society for boys called the Order of New Century Knighthood. He was honored as chaplain of the Missouri Senate and served as chaplain of the Missouri state penitentiary. While he did not necessarily regard the clientele of the two institutions as synonymous, he did feel that the Prohibition Party was the best kind of politics.

It took three ballots to choose the presidential nominee. In the early rounds, Palmore led and nearly obtained a majority. But on the third ballot, a "dark horse" emerged in the person of Eugene W. Chafin of Wisconsin. He had been active in many temperance activities as president of the state Epworth League, a high official in the Good Templars, and superintendent of the Washingtonian Home for inebriates in Chicago. He had written several successful histories such as **Lives of the Presidents** and **Washington as a Statesman.** Best known, however, was **Lincoln, the Man of Sorrow.**

Chafin was a strong believer in action on the local level. He was president for three terms of his county Agricultural Society. He was elected to a wide variety of local offices from police magistrate to the school board. To him, prohibition was only "one per cent legislation and ninety-nine per cent enforcement." In Chafin, the party found a vigorous opponent of the drift toward pragmatism.

The non-partisan temperance movement was placing too much emphasis on law without enforcement machinery. Chafin's largest salvos were leveled at the Anti-Saloon League. The League was endorsing any candidate for office who would vote correctly on the single issue of prohibition, irregardless of their views on other issues or Christian social justice. Their highly paid speakers were even exploiting Southern racism. Prohibition was being presented as another way of keeping the Negro in his place. Chafin declared angrily, "We have got to kill the Anti-Saloon League and then lick the Republican and Democratic parties."

When the Eighteenth Amendment was adopted, Chafin lay on his death bed. Friends who had worked with him for a lifetime in the cause gathered around him to celebrate. But Chafin shook his head. He predicted that the Volstead Act would prove in the end to be a bi-partisan conspiracy to discredit the legitimate temperance movement by non-enforcement of a law which the major parties really opposed. Before he died, he prophesied to them than the Eighteenth Amendment would be repealed in fifteen years and that the efforts of a century would have to be done all over again. As it turned out, it took only thirteen years.

Chafin's vice presidential running mate was Aaron S. Watkins. A Methodist minister and, like Chafin, a lawyer, Watkins was also a professor and officer of Ohio Northern University for many years. Later, he served as president of Asbury College in Kentucky.

Both Chafin and Watkins campaigned actively in twenty-eight states. The vote declined slightly to 253,231.

After the election, the party received a good deal of publicity from debates. The best known one began when the mayor of Milwaukee delivered an attack on the party and threw down the gauntlet for a debate. Samuel Dickie accepted the challenge and three debates were scheduled. But the first two were such an unequal contest that the mayor declined to appear in the third. The arguments were widely circulated in book form.

The party set up the Associated Prohibition Press, a bureau which sent out a constant stream of press releases, not only of the party but of non-partisan compaigns as well. Another active auxiliary to party work was the Woman's Prohibition Club of America. In 1909, thirty party members joined some 300 delegates from other countries at London to form the International Prohibition Confederation, later called the World Prohibition Federation.

Between presidential elections, mayors were elected in Fairmount, West Virginia, and Cortland, New York. The party elected one member to the Illinois legislature, besides the Minnesota victories noted previously. There were also many local officials elected around the country. Among the gubernatorial candidates was Andrew Jackson Houston of Texas, son of the famous Sam Houston.

Delegates from forty-two states convened on the Steel Pier, Atlantic City, New Jersey, in 1912. Among the convention officers was C. O. Fenton, editor of the **Times** of Logansport, Indiana. Clinton Howard, "the Little Giant" from Rochester, New York, was the keynote orator. He stirred the 900 delegates to shout an "Amen" with his speech depicting the Prohibition Party as the true Progressive party of that election. He wondered how Roosevelt could talk about voting theft, when he had stolen the Panama Canal Zone. Howard went on to list the big-city bosses who were backing Roosevelt, characterizing one of them as "the vice protector and promoter of Pittsburgh".

The party did face the same kind of insurgent unrest which was sweeping the other parties. A spirited struggle developed over the post of national chairman. The incumbent, Charles R. Jones of Illinois, was challenged by insurgent champion, W. G. Calderwood of Minnesota. A compromise was reached when Virgil G. Hinshaw of Portland, Oregon, was chosen.

A brief but comprehensive, 425-word platform was drafted. International arbitration of disputes appeared as before. Recall was added to initiative and referendum. To the previous stand on the postal system was added the advocacy of rural delivery and parcel post. The platform called for a single presidential term of six years. Besides its usual conservation plank, the party further called on the government to hold on to its mineral, timber, and water sites. If used, they should be leased for revenue. Rev. S. H. Taft of California proposed that the party change its name to Conservation Party. But there was so much opposition expressed that a vote was not taken.

For the first time in the party's history, the candidates of the previous election were renominated. Eugene Chafin and Aaron Watkins had not stopped campaigning in 1908. They had been speaking actively for four years. However, both had opposition for renomination. Chafin had four opponents, but won on the first ballot. When Andrew J. Houston, one of them, stood before the convention to withdraw, he drew cheers when he declared that he would rather have the lowest vote at a Prohibition convention than the highest vote at either convention of the major parties. Watkins was also renominated on the first ballot over two opponents.

During fourteen weeks of the 1912 campaign, Chafin made 538 speeches, averaging better than five per day. There were also vigorous local campaigns. Dr. Ivan D. Mishoff, a Bulgarian Orthodox immigrant, ran for mayor of Milwaukee, polling 1,200 votes in active campaigning. The Missouri candidate for governor had been elected mayor of Dexter, Missouri, three times and was the founding editor of the city's two newspapers. Daniel A. Poling waged an extensive campaign by automobile in his bid for governor of Ohio.

Dr. Poling, then a young party leader, went on to edit the **Christian Herald** for many years. He served as honorary life president of the World's Christian Endeavor, in recognition of his many years of service to that organization. He also served as president of the General Synod of the Reformed Church in America, and was author of twenty-six books. He was a chaplain and war correspondent in World War I. In later years, he was chaplain of the Inter-Faith Shrine in Philadelphia, a memorial to his son and three other chaplains who voluntarily went down with the "Dorchester" in World War II that others might have their places on the lifeboats.

In spite of the strong 1912 effort of the national ticket and the prestigious state tickets, the vote continued to decline. Chafin and Watkins polled 207,828 votes.

The National Committee set up its most ambitious program yet seen, after the 1912 election. It proposed raising one million dollars by the close of the 1916 campaign. By 1914, they had raised $250,000 and the state organizations had raised a similar amount. Secondly, the committee was to concentrate on not more than ten Congressional districts in 1914 for the purpose of winning. By 1916 they planned to have five million voters enrolled in the party.

In the 1914 race for United States Senator in Arizona, Eugene W. Chafin ran second. In Oregon's second Congressional district, a Prohibitionist ran a close second and nearly won in a three-way race, polling more than a third of the vote.

Party activity had been growing for several years in Oregon. The United States Senatorial candidate had made more than 250 speeches. There were nearly 1,000 volunteer workers, and more than 500,000 pieces of literature were distributed. Twenty of thirty-four counties were organized. In six counties, special efforts were made and 25% of the vote was captured. Several local and county candidates were elected and a legislative candidate missed election by only fourteen votes.

The number of registered Prohibitionists increased eight times over by 1914. This time, one legislative candidate won election. But there were even more near-wins. Six legislative candidates and two for sheriff came very close to victory. The candidate for State Treasurer polled 70,000 votes.

In New York, the American Party joined a coalition with the Prohibitionists to elect William Sulzer governor. Sulzer, who had formerly served as governor, polled 126,270 votes. In Minnesota, there were the seven legislative victories already noted. In Gloucester County, New Jersey, nine local candidates won. In Pennsylvania's Twenty-eighth Congressional district, the Prohibition candidate fell 3,000 votes short of election. Valentine A. Schreiber, Prohibition mayor of East Liverpool, Ohio, also ran a strong Congressional race.

In Los Angeles, Prohibitionists won their biggest victory by electing Charles H. Randall to Congress. Randall had been a journalist for many years. A Nebraska native, he began as editor of **The Observer** of Kimball, Nebraska. Thereafter, he edited several weekly newspapers. Moving to Los Angeles, he edited Highland Park's **California Herald** for many years. Affiliating with the Prohibition Party, he served on the Municipal Park Commission and served a term in the lower house of the California legislature. He served on the Los Angeles city council for ten years, part of the time as president. He was supported in 1914 by the Prohibition and Democratic parties for Congress.

A group of forty college students from the Intercollegiate Prohibition Association spent their summer vacation canvassing door-to-door. They enrolled almost 20,000 voters for the party. Randall's vote was 27,500. He went on to serve two more terms in the United States House of Representatives. In his final two terms, he had the endorsement of the Republican, Progressive, Democratic and Prohibition parties. While in Congress, he sponsored a number of the leading laws for the restriction of the liquor traffic, including the rider which created war-time prohibition. However, he voted against American entry into the war.

As the 1916 campaign approached, the Anti-Saloon League began to endorse far stronger temperance measures than previously. The League had generally supported the Republican Party, but now Prohibitionists were given more prominent positions in this and other temperance organizations of a non-partisan nature. Party members were important in the Committee of Sixty on National Prohibition, which was so important in pressuring Congress and the various party platform committees. Partisans were also numerous among the speakers of the Flying Squadron of America, formed to barnstorm the country with fiery orations to build grassroots support for national prohibition.

The Flying Squadron was headed by J. Frank Hanly, former governor of Indiana. Hanly began as a teacher and lawyer. He rose through the ranks of the Republican Party as a state Senator and Congressman for one term. During his single term as governor of Indiana, he promoted various reforms, particularly temperance legislation. Although a popular vote-getter, he was barred by law from succeeding himself. The Republicans were defeated in the next election with the liquor traffic as the chief issue. Thereafter, his party ostracized him and he adhered to the Prohibitionists. He founded and edited the **National Enquirer.** He was also editor of the **Indianapolis Daily Commercial.** He was famous for his speech, "I Hate It," an eloquent attack on the liquor traffic which has often been quoted.

The Prohibition national convention of 1916 was held in St. Paul, Minnesota. Daniel Poling delivered the keynote address, "Save America and Serve the World." The three presidential candidates were all former governors: Sulzer of New York, Foss of Massachusetts, and Hanly of Indiana. J. Frank Hanly was the first-ballot winner.

To balance the ticket, a Southern Democratic convert was named for vice president. Ira Landrith was editor of **The Cumberland Presbyterian** in Nashville, Tennessee, and moderator of his church's General Assembly. For many years, he headed the Tennessee YMCA and had been president of the International YMCA Convention. Among other honors, he was chairman of the Committee of 100 which brought reform to the Nashville city government, general secretary of the Religious Education Association, editor afield and extension secretary of the Christian Endeavor, an officer in the Anti-Saloon League, and president of Ward Seminary and Bellmont College.

In contrast to the previous two platforms, the one in 1916 was the longest ever. It called on the four million women then voting to reward the party which had always championed their cause.

It condemned militarism and "the wasteful military program" of the two major parties. The party called for a World Court to settle international disputes, "maintained as to give its decrees binding force." While they did wish military protection of a strictly defensive nature, they called for international disarmament agreements. Profiteering and fraud in military manufacturing were condemned. In peacetime, the army should be used in conservation projects and highway construction. An inland waterway from Florida to Maine was particularly suggested.

The platform pointed out that the Monroe Doctrine was not only a privilege but a responsibility. Conquest and exploitation were condemned, particularly in Mexico, although the general principle of the Monroe Doctrine was upheld.

The platform called for the independence of the Philippines as soon as they had been properly prepared. Reciprocal trade agreements were specifically called for. Several proposals were made to strengthen our merchant marine, including government subsidies for mail and other services.

In Civil Service, they urged closer watch of demotions and removals by a non-partisan commission. The merit system should be extended to postmasters, revenue collectors and marshals. Government employers should also have tenure and a retirement and disability system.

To the usual labor benefits were added the endorsement of the eight-hour working day and sanitary working conditions. Another plank called for a system of old-age pensions and unemployment insurance. For the farmer, the party urged government ownership of grain elevators and other marketing facilities. Furthermore, a federal inspection system under Civil Service should be set up to prevent manipulations and speculations on the market price of farm products by private business groups. The cooperative movement was also endorsed. Government ownership of public utilities or "natural monopolies" was urged.

The platform urged that the itemized veto on appropriation bills should be granted as a power of the President. "Pork barrel" legislation was condemned. Declaring America to be "the land of all peoples and belongs not to any one," the party called for federal action for settling immigrants in vocations and situations which would best acclimate them to their new land. The platform concluded by accusing the two major parties of being in reality a single "Conservative party." The Prohibition Party declared itself to be the only true representative of the Progressive spirit in 1916.

From the St. John campaign until the death of Frances Willard, the National WCTU had always endorsed the Prohibition Party. After Miss Willard passed from the scene, the WCTU became non-partisan and pragmatic under the influence of the Anti-Saloon League. In 1916, they broke with this policy briefly and again endorsed the Prohibition ticket.

Another aid to the party was the ability to finance a special campaign train once again. Beginning in Chicago, the whistlestop went to the Pacific coast, from there to the Atlantic and back to Chicago again. It covered nearly 20,000 miles in thirty-four states. Hanly and Landrith held from five to fifteen meetings per day in this manner.

It was a pragmatic campaign, however, centering on the success of state referendums for prohibitory amendments. The party was being used once again by the candidates as a pressure on the major parties to gain legislation on a single issue. A party vote and a party for comprehensive Christian change was de-emphasized.

The party was on the ballot in forty-four states. However, there was only a slight increase in the returns. Hanly and Landrith polled 221,329 votes. In five states alone, the state tickets ran ahead of the national vote by 183,000.

In Florida, the Prohibition Party scored a big victory. Sidney J. Catts, the party candidate for governor, was elected. The Minnesota candidate for United States Senator polled 78,426 votes.

In New York, Dr. C. E. Welch was the candidate for governor. Welch, originally a New Jersey dentist, had tried to persuade his Methodist conference to stop serving wine for communion. He developed a grape juice which was free of bacteria. Promoting it in the churches for sacramental purposes, he soon developed a family business. Moving to New York, he greatly expanded the sale of Welch's Grape Juice through exhibitions at the world fairs and a national advertising campaign. (The girls in the ads said: "My lips only touch lips that touch Welch's.") His discovery was widely promoted by such temperance leaders as William Jennings Bryan, and Welch's Grape Juice became a national drink. Dr. Welch was elected six times as village president of Westfield, New York.

By 1918, the party's national chairman reported that he had "adjourned politics," working for the election of "dry" legislators regardless of party. Special state editions of the party's paper, **Patriot Phalanx,** went to one million homes in twelve states where there were ratification fights for prohibition. All sorts of other methods of pressure politics were used. Daniel Poling headed the United Committee for War Temperance Activities which carried on temperance education in the Army and Navy. Prohibitionists were even active in an unsuccessful effort to get the major parties to pledge prohibition enforcement in their 1920 platforms.

Lincoln, Nebraska, was the site of the 1920 Prohibition convention. The refusal of the major parties to promise enforcement of the Eighteenth Amendment gave the party added impetus. For many years, the party's symbol had been the white rose. As early as 1912, a dromedary camel was used on party campaign pins. At the 1920 convention, the bactrian (two-humped) camel was selected to stress the party's "dry" traditions. The bactrian camel was the animal best suited to lead America through a dry and thirsty land.

The convention's presiding officer was Miss Marie C. Brehm, the first woman to hold such a position in American history. A major figure in the woman suffrage movement, she had been superintendent of the franchise department of the National WCTU, the largest organization working for woman suffrage. She had also served as president of the Equal Suffrage Association of Illinois. Miss Brehm was President Wilson's delegate to the World's Anti-Alcohol Convention in Milan, Italy, in spite of her long affiliation with the Prohibition Party as a candidate for statewide offices.

The platform called for an immediate ratification of the peace treaty. While it did not object to "reasonable reservations," the United States was urged to join the League of Nations. "The time is past when the United States can hold aloof from the affairs of the world. Such a course is short-sighted and only invites disaster." The party further called for a constitutional amendment to permit Congressional ratification of peace treaties by a simple majority of both houses.

State supervision of parochial schools was urged to insure an equal quality of education and that such education be in the English language. The program of the National League of Women Voters was incorporated wholly into the platform: setting up a Children's Bureau, a federal program for maternity and infant care, a federal department of education with federal aid for teachers' salaries and literacy programs, citizenship training of youths and immigrants, home economics vocational training, federal supervision of the marketing and distribution of food, a Woman's Bureau of the Department of Labor to improve working conditions of women, appointment of women to mediation boards, a joint federal and state employment service, sex education in the schools and a campaign against venereal disease.

Industrial courts were called for as a means of settling labor disputes. They pledged to eliminate excessive profiteering and "all unnecessary middlemen." Those involved in interstate commerce would be prevented from practices which amounted to extortion, such as tying contracts (forcing an unwanted article upon the buyer as a condition for purchasing a desired article). Such corporations would be required to reveal the difference between actual cost and the price. There were the usual pledges to the farmer as well.

The platform included a plank on presidential qualifications. The party stated that unwritten qualifications of moral example were more important than written ones. They said further that lawlessness was a "crying evil of the day." Prohibitionists concluded that their party had "never sold its birthright for a mess of pottage."

For president, the delegates returned to a party regular, Aaron S. Watkins. D. Leigh Colvin was named as vice presidential candidate. He had been president for sixteen years of the Intercollegiate Prohibition Association. He was an officer in almost every temperance organization on the national and world scene, and he was one of the most widely travelled men in the party.

He had spoken at more than 400 European and American colleges and universities. Both he and his wife, Mamie W. Colvin, held doctoral degrees from Columbia University. Mrs. Colvin was for many years president of the National WCTU and a member of the Women's Advisory Committee of the United States Army. Both she and her husband served the party as candidates over many years of campaigning. Dr. Colvin wrote a history of the Prohibition Party which has been the party's standard source of information ever since.

By 1920, the opportunists who had never understood the full vision of the party were deserting the cause in droves. State organizations were disintegrating as many leaders regarded the party's objectives complete, merely because there were laws on the books. The result was that the party was on the ballot in only twenty-five states compared with forty-four in the previous campaign.

Watkins and Colvin campaigned extensively from coast to coast. Surprisingly enough, the popular vote among grassroots supporters held up enough to be comparable to earlier campaigns, despite the reduced number of states permitting returns. Watkins and Colvin received 195,923 votes. Two women seeking seats in the United States Senate also added to party laurels. Mrs. Ella A. Boole, National WCTU president, polled 159,477 votes in New York, while Mrs. Leah Cobb Marion polled 132,610 votes in Pennsylvaina.

CHAPTER VII

IN AND OUT OF THE CHASM, 1920-1932

During the decade following World War I, the two major parties began to make moves to bar minor parties from the ballot. It was a trend unprecedented in American history, but it was a trend which would grip national politics with increasing pressure down to the present day.

The two parties wanted to make sure that there would never again be an outpouring of humanitarian reform comparable to that of the Progressive Era. From then on, they could be in the comfortable position of joining hands in a conspiracy of silence on the issues that really mattered. The technique was to create ballot laws which were so stringent that a dissenting group would have to expend all of its resources obtaining a place on the ballot, and have nothing left with which to campaign. By 1924, the Prohibition Party could only obtain returns from sixteen states.

In that year, the national convention met in early June at Columbus, Ohio. Most of the pragmatists were gone, but there were some delegates who had come to the convention for the purpose of voting the party out of existence. However, those of the prophetic tradition prevailed.

For the first time in many years, the platform specifically proclaimed Christianity as the guide to its principles. It soundly condemned the corruption and "moral bankruptcy" of the Harding-Coolidge administration. The Teapot Dome scandal was attacked in a plank on conservation. Concern was expressed about unassimilated immigrants. The rest of the platform read much the same as it had four years before.

Herman P. Faris was named as presidential candidate. Faris was a leading Missouri businessman who was an officer and the manager of Brinkerhoff-Faris Trust and Savings Company. Prominent in land dealings, he was president and manager of Clinton Reality Company and Brinton Land Company. He was three times commander of the General Assembly of Woodsmen.

Marie C. Brehm was honored with a second distinction for womanhood. She was nominated for vice president and became the first woman to have her name placed on official ballots for nation-wide office. There had been a couple of token candidates for president in the previous century. But their activities had been either eccentric or ineffectual in terms of votes. Miss Brehm was the first woman to be nominated by a serious party and the first to receive recordable votes. Faris and Brehm polled 56,289 votes.

In 1926, the Prohibition Party was supported by a coalition of other church and temperance groups to defeat a "wet" Republican, Senator James W. Wadsworth, Jr. Enough votes were polled to cause his defeat. (He entered the lower house in Congress several years later, where he co-sponsored the first peacetime draft, the Burke-Wadsworth Act of 1940. His son-in-law, Stuart Symington, has served in the Senate for many years and a grandson is also serving in Congress.

The darkest, loneliest days of the Prohibition Party lay in the years ahead. In 1928, fear of Roman Catholicism and a "wet" victory swept through the Protestant churches. To many, Herbert Hoover and the Republican pledge to support prohibition made the choice clear enough, with Al Smith as the Democratic nominee. There was nothing unusual about northern Protestants reacting in this way. Most of them had been buying the Republican line for generations. What was unusual was that Prohibition leaders also panicked.

Ever since the Eighteenth Amendment and the Volstead Act, those who had remained in the Prohibition Party had maintained that all of the reforms of the Progressive Era would be lost if the two-party system of the old politics continued to be perpetuated. Laws on the books without the moral fiber to enforce them would ultimately result in failure. Now, even these loyalists were stampeded by the specter of Al Smith.

One man among them stood virtually alone. William F. Varney wanted to carry on if the rest did not, and so they let him. Varney had been a long-time party regular who had directed the election victories of 1914 in Gloucester County, New Jersey. He had been a successful business manager in the textile industry of New Jersey and New York. He was manager of Wright, Veith and Newman, making pillow shams and scarfs. Later, he managed Stahli, Reitmann and Company, making curtains and novelties.

The quadrennial convention gathered in Chicago in 1928. Many delegates wanted to endorse Herbert Hoover and there was a heated debate. However, a liberal platform was drafted and William F. Varney was nominated for president. The California delegation refused to support the national ticket and Herbert Hoover's name was carried at the head of the Prohibition ticket in California.

The regular vice presidential candidate was James A. Edgerton. Edgerton was a poet and philosopher who had written eleven books. He was president of the National, and later, the International New Thought Alliance. In his early career, he had edited several local and county newspapers on the Nebraska frontier. He served as state chairman of the Populist Party, as secretary of the party's national committee, and as the party's nominee for clerk of the United States House of Representatives.

Edgerton went on to a long record of government service. He was secretary of the Nebraska State Labor Bureau. Moving into federal service, he was purchasing agent for the Post Office Department. During World War I, he was a member of the War Industries Board. Thereafter, he was federal prohibition enforcement director for New Jersey.

Varney and Edgerton had to campaign virtually alone. Even the national chairman and much of the party's regular organization did not assist them. They were able to secure a place on the ballot in only six states, receiving 20,106 votes. The Hoover Prohibition ticket polled another 14,394 votes in California. In Pennsylvania, 14,866 voters cast a Prohibition ticket only to find that their leaders had left the box for presidential electors blank. Thus while the showing appeared to be disastrous, the vote totals compared favorably with previous returns in the states where the party was on the ballot.

The enactment of prohibition nearly caused the death of the Prohibition Party. Repeal of prohibition brought it back to life again. By 1932, many "drys" were feeling once more that the major parties had betrayed them. The vote for state candidates was pushed to record levels. Had circumstances been different, the support might have been translated into a large presidential vote as well.

In California, Miss M. L. Hutchins polled 152,000 votes for Secretary of State in 1930. Dr. Hutchins, who began as a teacher, was one of the pioneering women to enter the field of medicine in frontier days. California Republicans in 1932 nominated a "wet" for the United States Senate. The majority of the state's rank-and-file Republicans rallied behind the Prohibition Senatorial candidate, Robert F. Schuler. Schuler was a widely-known Methodist clergyman of Los Angeles and editor of one of that church's leading periodicals. Schuler ran second in the election, polling 560,088 votes. He set the all-time record as a Prohibition vote-getter. "Dry" Democrat William Gibbs McAdoo was elected and the Republican candidate ran a poor third.

In Pennsylvania, Gifford Pinchot had received much attention during an earlier term as Republican governor. During his first term (1923-1927), he had courageously exposed the Republican administration in Washington when it licensed breweries in Pennsylvania which the state laws were trying to suppress. In 1930, he sought to make a come-back by seeking the Prohibition primary nomination as well as that of his own party. He won both nominations for governor. Pennsylvania Prohibitionists delivered 31,909 votes in a very close race. Their support proved to be crucial in electing Pinchot as governor. His vigorous policies in fighting the Great Depression are still remembered by Pennsylvania's many "Pinchot roads."

Pinchot, educated in European forestry methods, was America's first professionally trained forester. He had been in charge of the National Forest Service, responsible for Theodore Roosevelt's conservation program. He had been a member of the National Forest Commission and the Inland Waterways Commission. He served as chairman of the National Conservation Commission and as president of the National Conservation Association.

By 1931, Pennsylvania's Prohibition Party had become a factor once again in state politics. In a special election for United States Senator, Mrs. Mabel D. Pennock captured 143,000 ballots. The regular candidate polled 106,597 votes for the office the following year. He was Dr. Edward J. Fithian, a businessman with 1,700 employees. The 1932 California and Pennsylvania Senatorial totals alone pushed the party vote far beyond any previous showings, not to mention the increased vote in so many other states.

Prohibitionists gathered for their national convention of 1932 in Indianapolis. There was hope that the growing disillusionment of "drys" could be translated into a large presidential vote. They met after the two major parties, both of which endorsed resubmission of prohibition.

The platform which was drafted was very similar to that of 1928 with the addition of several proposals to alleviate the Great Depression. It proposed that the federal government buy state and municipal bonds. In the depths of the Depression, these governments were facing heavy expenses, yet they found it difficult to market bonds. The party proposed that the federal government buy these bonds and use them as collateral to issue more currency, which was also in short supply.

As other methods of dealing with the crisis, they proposed the creation of an economic council, federal regulation of the stock exchanges and boards of trade, minimum wage and maximum hour laws, tariff revisions, insurance of bank deposits, relief and unemployment insurance, plus a more honest assessment of industrial properties for taxation. In agriculture, they endorsed an equalization fee. They called for judicial reforms, such as curbing the powers of injunction. Strict federal censorship of movies was called for. Representation in legislative bodies should be apportioned on the number of citizens, not merely on census figures which include aliens. Public ownership of public utilities was endorsed.

There was widespread dissatisfaction with the national chairman, Dr. Colvin, due to his lack of support for the national ticket in the previous election. The convention did not, however, wish to undermine some delicate negotiations which he had been carrying on for some time with Senator William E. Borah of Idaho. The hope was that Borah would consent to be the party's presidential nominee. He was willing if disaffected groups could be enlisted from the major parties. The convention nominated him by acclamation. A committee was elected to talk with him directly by telephone. But he would not accept or decline the nomination.

The convention decided to name candidates pledged to withdraw in case Senator Borah consented to run. They turned to William D. Upshaw of Georgia. Upshaw spent his youth struggling against the handicap of being unable to walk due to injury in a fall. He earned money lecturing from a rolling chair, and his autobiography went through eleven editions. Early in the twentieth century, he founded and edited a magazine, **The Golden Age,** in Atlanta, Georgia. Beginning in 1919, he served four terms as Democratic Congressman from Georgia, noted especially for his championing the cause of organized labor during these lean years for unions. He also served as a member of the Scandinavian Commercial Commission. He left his party when it became clear that it was not supporting prohibition in 1928.

For vice president, Frank S. Regan was named. Regan, editor of **The Taxpayer,** had been a Lyceum cartoonist-lecturer. He could deliver illustrated lectures with rapid crayon work and served on the Chautauqua circuit for twenty-two years. In Rockford, Illinois, he won a seat on the board of aldermen as a Prohibitionist. By 1898, he was able to win a seat in the Illinois legislature where he cast the deciding vote on four legislative questions.

Senator Borah kept the party on the string for a long time. His final decision was to decline the nomination. The uncertainty greatly crippled the campaign and made it difficult to transform the swelling support for local tickets into a large presidential vote. Upshaw and Regan won 81,869 votes in twenty-two states. If the vote were calculated by the top vote-getter in each state in 1932, the total comes to over three-quarters of a million. The Senatorial candidate in Ohio alone polled 36,000, and the Virginia candidate for Congressman-at-large received another 16,000 votes. This was in addition to the turnout in California and Pennsylvania as noted above.

CHAPTER VIII

SEEKING A NEW DIRECTION, 1932-1944

Shortly after the election of 1932, a new national chairman assumed the party's leadership in the person of Edward Blake. **The National Prohibitionist** was again launched in March of 1933. The paper, published in Chicago, printed several exposés on the corruption and gangsters in the city. It soon attracted a broad base of local support for the party.

When 325 delegates met in December at the Cook County Prohibition Convention, forty-four of the city's fifty wards had been organized, as well as nine of the county's outlying towns. Crime and municipal corruption were the key issues enunciated. Jewish voters and some Roman Catholics were recruited in ward caucuses. One ward chairman was an Irish-born, reformed barmaid. But the party's strongest support came from Negro wards. Rev. Lewis G. Jordan, a nationally-known evangelist was particularly active. Another important figure over many years of party activity was Mrs. Ida B. Thompson. Mrs. Thompson was the widow of a pioneering Negro judge and a teacher in her own right at several Negro schools of higher education.

The Chicago campaigns produced some of the most colorful coalitions in the party's history. John Harper was a native of Scotland's Orkney Islands and sold tailor supplies to members of that trade around the country. A. W. Fairbanks was a printer and a resident of Hull House. Dr. Newton G. Thomas was dean of Illinois University's Dental School.

Illinois state activity began to revive also. County conventions were held all over the state with increased attendance. Party leaders around the country began to note that half of the delegates at state and local conventions were new members. In West Virginia, 70% of the delegates at the state convention were new-comers. In a series of meetings in Kentucky, William Upshaw drew between one and two thousand listeners per day. The Pennsylvania state chairman reported automobile mileage of 20,777 miles for the year ending July, 1933.

As it became clearer that the Twenty-first Amendment would be adopted, there was a feeling of betrayal. Those "drys" who were not dispirited began to renounce their old party ties. Several newspapermen and printers were won to the party in various states. C. J. Millington, municipal judge of Cadillac, Michigan, endorsed the party. So did Miss Belle Kearney, Mississippi state Senator and a leader in national Democratic women's activities.

Religious groups also began to endorse the party. The Idaho-Oregon Nazarene Assembly and the Oregon Society of Friends specifically endorsed the party. The president of the Unitarian Fellowship for Social Justice joined in party activities. Other groups endorsed the idea of a new party, although they would not mention the Prohibition Party by name. This was the case with the National WCTU and the Central New York Methodist Conference.

The party was also encouraged by the many distinguished members of yesteryear, such as Charles M. Sheldon. As editor-in-chief of the **Christian Herald,** he had been an associate of Daniel Poling who later succeeded him in that capacity. The party's new chaiman, Edward Blake, was also an old associate. Sheldon was the author of more than thirty books and editor of a dozen more, including **All Over Forty** which he adapted for a motion picture.

Sheldon received much attention by accepting the challenge of the **Topeka Capital** to run the newspaper for a week without liquor advertising. He was a smashing success. But his greatest achievement was an 1896 novel, **In His Steps.** Revised twice in the 1920's, it was the biggest sensation in print during the decade. It still holds the all-time record as the best-selling novel, having sold more than twenty-five mlilion copies in twenty-one languages. In it, he asked the question, "What Would Jesus Do?" In politics, Sheldon believed that the answer to that question was the Prohibition Party.

Party leaders began to feel that a change of name would better suggest the comprehensive views of the party. On the eve of the 1934 elections, the **National Prohibitionist** was full of letters debating the idea. There were already groups in various places who agreed with the Prohibition Party, wished to join forces with it, but who were operating under different names. In Connecticut, the Independent Republican Party's Milton C. Conover, a Yale professor, had polled enough votes to prevent the election of a "wet" Republican to the United States Senate. In Rockville Center, New York, William Varney came very close to winning as mayor on the Home Protection Party label, polling 2,547 votes. Already, a group of prominent New York citizens had formed the Law Preservation Party and were seeking to join forces.

The Prohibition Party in New York agreed to merge under the name, Law Preservation Party, with William Varney and Dr. D. Leigh Colvin playing important roles. In Michigan, a Citizens Committee delegation attended the state convention, wishing to embrace the party if a different name were chosen. In spite of the fact that this committee represented a small minority of those present, the name was changed to Commonwealth Party. In Ohio, a similar effort was made. However, over 200 delegates of the Prohibition Party appeared, while only sixty-four members of the Commonwealth Party attended. When the Prohibitionists refused to change their name the two groups went their separate ways. In Iowa, the Union Party label was suggested, but no action was taken. Massachusetts flatly rejected the Commonwealth proposal.

The platforms of 1934 were full of the usual new ideas. The Virginia platform condemned the lay-offs and pay-cuts of federal employees and opposed the short ballot movement as undemocratic. Massachusetts called for prison reform under the Norfolk Colony Plan. Indiana wanted the abolition of all munitions manufacturing by private firms.

Oklahoma called for consolidation of county and local governments. They endorsed the program of the Farmer's Union, and held that sales and income taxes were preferable to the property tax on farms. In Illinois, however, the sales tax was opposed and a property tax on the full value of industries was endorsed as adequate. Frank Regan was particularly active in promoting the one per cent limit on all taxes. Illinois Prohibitionists saw solutions for the Depression in suspension of mortgage foreclosures, a promotion of public works, and the city manager form of government to eliminate the costs of graft.

Even prior to the general state elections of 1934, there were signs of strength in local elections. In Gettysburg, Ohio, a mayor and three councelors were elected giving the Prohibition Party control of the city. Three other officials were elected there, plus two near-wins.

The fall elections revealed that 244,597 voters had supported the candidate running at the top of the ballot in sixteen states. 176,276 of these votes came from California. The total of the highest vote-getter in each state was 487,840 votes, of which 396,852 came from California. Most of the rest came from Massachusetts, Pennsylvania and New York. New York's Law Preservation Party did comparatively well. Varney received 20,499 votes for governor there.

It was, however, in Michigan where the deepest impression would be made in relation to a change of name. The old party had been controlled by more liberal Easterners belonging to mainstream Protestant denominations. The new party was far more an organization of Midwestern fundamentalists who belonged to splinter denominations. These people had been in the party since the earliest days, but had not previously been able to dominate the party as they now could. Therefore, it was in Michigan where any name-change would have to prove itself. The Commonwealth Party, however, met with disaster at the polls. Rank-and-file partisans, who in earlier periods had supported liberal leadership, began to demonstrate that they were going to rule the party now in a more fundamentalist style. The Prohibition vote in 1932 had been 2,031. In 1934, the Commonwealth vote dropped to 800. Nor did it even hold at this low level. In spite of determined Commonwealth campaigns, the vote dropped to 433 in 1936 and to 242 in 1938. By 1940, the party had lost the ballot altogether. A broader-based leadership had alienated the Prohibitionists while failing to deliver any new group of voters to the movement.

The dilemma of a name change had been dramatized. Groups which said they would support a party with a different name had been unsuccessful in producing large crowds at meetings or a large turn-out at the polls. Most people who said that they did not like the Prohibition label just were not interested in voting for any minor party anyway. On the other hand, the party did not have the resources to sell a new name to those who were party regulars. Many Prohibitionists of the prophetic tradition were suspicious of any change as a sign of softness, while others simply were not informed of it. Many, when taking their ballot and not seeing their old party name there, simply assumed that it was gone. The party enjoyed the support at the polls of many who never kept any direct contact with the organized effort. A good example was Robert Benchley, dramatic critic for **Life** magazine and the **New Yorker.** The witty author of five best-sellers, he starred in several comedy roles in Hollywood movies. Except for a brief time in his youth he took no part in Prohibition Party activities and the party lost contact with him. It was not until after his death that the party would discover that he had been one of its supporters at the polls.

The controversy over a name change continued on into the 1936 campaign. Michigan remained loyal to the Commonwealth name and Maine also adopted it after twenty years of partisan inactivity there. In Ohio, party regulars were defeated by one vote with most delegates abstaining. A committee was chosen to negotiate a union with the Commonwealth Party. However, the Prohibition name was kept after the deliberations were complete.

The Prohibition national convention was held at Niagara Falls, New York, with about 200 delegates from twenty-five states. The platform committee reported favorably on changing the national name to Commonwealth. The proposal was defeated and the entire platform report was revised. Will D. Martin was the Resolutions chairman. He was manager of the Hasbrouck Heights (New Jersey) Building operated by that town's

Savings and Loan Association. He had also been a local office-holder, including a term as president of the Hasbrouck Heights Board of Education. Martin defended the comprehensive platform with fair success. The final version of the platform was not much different from that of 1932. However, it did not call for government ownership of public utilities and other strongly socialistic planks of earlier years. Its currency plank was slightly more moderate but with much the same wording. Communism and Fascism in the United States were condemned. Reform of the "antiquated and out-moded system of judicial procedure" was called for. The Colorado state platform had endorsed the Townsend Plan, but this was not adopted in the national platform.

A highlight of the convention was a National Youth Dinner and the launching of a party youth organization. The convention also paid special tribute to the passing of Father George Zurcher, long the key Roman Catholic leader in the party. Father John Kubacki, Indiana delegate, led in the eulogies.

The convention chairman was Harold C. Mason, president of Huntington College. He had also served as dean of Adrian College and was a bishop in the United Brethren Church. The deliberations received wide publicity. Newsreels with sound were taken for theaters across the country. When the convention nominated Dr. D. Leigh Colvin for president, his addresses were broadcast nation-wide over radio.

Sergeant Alvin York, World War I hero lionized in book and film for his capture of an incredible number of German machine gunners, was nominated for vice president. He ultimately declined the honor and was replaced by Claude A. Watson. A Michigan native, Watson had been general manager of Four Drive Tractor Company. Moving to California, he became one of the foremost lawyers in Los Angeles, conducting the radio series entitled "Weekly Open Forum." He was district superintendent of the Free Methodist Church for twelve years and secretary of the Free Methodist Publishing House.

Prohibitionists were cheered by victories in Venango County, Pennsylvania. The fall elections of 1935 saw fourteen Prohibitionists elected there on their ticket alone. Another six won with the endorsement of another party besides their own. Six office-seekers of other parties also owed their election to votes received on the Prohibition ticket. The party had polled 25% of the vote county-wide (5,413).

Colvin and Watson waged the most extensive campaigns that the party had seen in sixteen years. Dr. Colvin travelled 27,000 miles, more than any other presidential candidate running that year. But the results were most disappointing. Dr. Colvin, the foremost advocate of a name change in the party, probably suffered at the hands of party regulars. Meantime, the Commonwealth idea was not producing results. Colvin's vote in Michigan was only 579, and the new name made little impression on Maine voters either (334 votes). In returns from twenty-five states, Colvin and Watson polled 37,847 votes.

The following year, the party entered the gubernatorial races of Virginia and New Jersey. In Virginia, James A. Edgerton campaigned against the poll tax as a requirement for voting. In both states, the candidates attacked political influence in the state parole systems. In the 1938 campaign, Michigan's Commonwealth Party rejected the Townsend Recovery Plan by a narrow margin.

The regular mid-term elections attracted some impressive candidates. Oklahoma's candidate for governor had been a missionary to India for thirteen years. Their Senatorial candidate was P. C. Nelson, author of several textbooks for Bible courses in higher education. Michigan's gubernatorial candidate was an Armenian nationalist driven from his native land by the Turks. In Kansas, C. Floyd Hester, president of Miltonvale's Wesleyan College, ran for governor.

One of the candidates for state-wide office in Georgia won 10% of the vote. The party had many enthusiastic meetings around the country. One of those active in organizing the work was Rev. Sam Morris of Texas, nationally-known radio comentator (Voice of Temperance). On September 1 and 2 of 1939, Prohibitionists gathered near Farewell Hall to observe the party's seventieth anniversary. Roger W. Babson took this occasion to make his dramatic announcement, broadcast over one of the national radio networks. He declared that he was joining the Prohibition Party.

Roger W. Babson began in 1903 with **Babson's Reports.** He became the pioneer in economic forecasting through a system of statistical analysis. It made him immensely wealthy, particularly after he was the only major economist to predict the 1929 Crash accurately. During World War I, Babson had served as Director of General Information and Education for the government.

He wrote thirty-seven books in the business field alone, plus religious and political works. He was an officer in several large businesses, including United Stores Corporation. He served a term as national moderator of the Congregational Christian Church. He was chairman of the Gravity Research Foundation which gave a good deal of money to college science programs around the country.

Babson founded three business schools: Babson Institute in Massachusetts, Webber College for women in Florida, and Midwest Institute in Kansas. Through his Business Statistics Organization at Babson Park, Massachusetts, with branches all over the world, he gave out his information on stock and business prospects in syndicated newspaper columns throughout the continent. But he always refused to advise clients to invest in the liquor industry, no matter how well the statistics indicated its prospects.

Mr. Babson was impressed by the fact that the party had used the word prohibition as a broad-based philosophy, not just something aimed at the liquor traffic. He urged that the attacks on the liquor industry be reduced in proportion to other evils in society.

One of the things he felt should be prohibited was political influence over the schools. He reasoned that athletics were being over-emphasized, and that scholastic standards were being lowered to graduate more pupils. He charged that firms selling school supplies were exerting undue pressure. He also opposed consolidation and bussing.

Another issue which Babson stressed often was limited franchise. He felt that voting should be restricted to those who were qualified. In Roger W. Babson, the party had found a leader who was far more conservative than any had been up to that time. Under his influence, state platforms, beginning with that of his own state of Florida, abandoned the specific, radical social reforms of the past. Platforms became more vague and platitudinous. The trend began to de-emphasize the liquor traffic as well. The Florida platform used the word "liquor" only once in listing ten commercialized evils to be prohibited. Illinois was one of the few states to adopt a broader platform. Along with the usual planks, the convention called for the outlawing of any political party which acted as an agent of any foreign government.

By the time of the national convention in Chicago (May, 1940), Babson was firmly in control. The platform, while implying support for the social issues of the past, was far less specific. Lewd literature, block booking of indecent movies, and deceptive radio broadcasting were among the evils to be prohibited. Equitable immigration and tariff policies were among the economic programs advocated. The platform called for a spiritual reawakening and a coalition of church people behind the New Prohibition Party. The newness was stressed throughout the campaign.

Party regulars were not wholly pleased with the platform. An effort was made to endorse the Townsend Plan and to adopt the old monetary plank. But these efforts were unsuccessful. The party chose instead to present itself as a conservative alternative. The "me-tooism" of Willkie had made both major parties equally liberal and this was stressed by the Prohibition candidates.

To no one's suprise, Roger W. Babson was nominated for president. His nomination elicited a very enthusiastic demonstration at the convention, which moved Babson to tears for the first time in his life "in public." For vice president, the delegates also named a new-comer and long-time Babson associate. Edgar V. Moorman was president of Moorman Manufacturing Company, the largest firm in Quincy, Illinois. His plant was a food processing industry. Around Quincy, Moorman owned large farms and experimental stations. He employed 400 workers and 2,000 salesmen around the country. He required that each worker be a member of some church, and for many years he had been the chief backer of Dr. E. Stanley Jones' mission in India.

Babson made two major campaign tours, one into the South and the other across the country to California. He travelled a total of 10,000 miles in thirty states. Everywhere he went, he was greeted by mayors, Chambers of Commerce, and civic groups at lavish banquets. Leading churches invited him in as they had not done for a Prohibition candidate in decades. Newspaper and radio interviews were made available to him on every hand. He received a number of honorary degrees during college engagements. It was a triumphal tour in honor of a retiring member of the business community. Moorman also appeared at some major campaign functions, especially in the Midwest.

Babson and Moorman received some support in the college community. A group of Williams College students worked for the ticket with particular interest. Dr. Ganfield, former president of Carroll College, and W. L. Jessup, president of San Jose Bible College, were active supporters. The Kansas candidate for United States Senator was William F. McConn, president of Marion College.

There were many radio broadcasts in the Babson campaign, including one nation-wide address over the Columbia Network. But while he was reaching many distinguished audiences, he was winning few of their votes. They were only listening respectfully without really responding, and he knew it. He noted that the chief concerns of those he met were the ominous events of World War II, not the need for moral rearmament at home. Yet he continued to emphasize that America's real hope lay in spiritual vision and moral strength. He predicted that even if Germany and Japan were completely destroyed, they would still rise to be our economic competitors in the post-war world because of the moral purpose of their people. Of course, he regarded their present leadership as entirely wrong, but he stressed that America would only win the economic race with them in the post-war world by a spiritual reawakening. Many people told him they agreed with him 100%, and then they would add that they would not vote for him in spite of it.

While he failed to persuade his new audiences, he also suffered at the hands of party stalwarts who did not like his de-emphasis of the liquor question and his conservative social views. Babson suggested that the party's coverage of issues be broadened in its newspaper and that the paper's name be changed. He advocated that the party name be changed to the Church Party, while Moorman suggested His Kingdom Party as a suitable name. On one occasion during the campaign, party leaders at a particular meeting were so cool toward Babson that he rented a hall across the street. When it came his turn to speak, he then invited all those who were supporting him to follow him over to the other hall.

Babson and Moorman won 59,492 votes in thirty-six states. However, eight of these states were reporting only a scattering of write-ins. The state tickets polled 454,418 votes. Most of the discrepancy with the national vote came from California, Kansas, Massachusetts and Pennsylvania. Charles H. Randall polled 22% of the vote as a California Congressional candidate in his old district. The Michigan vote tripled after its return to the Prohibition label.

The election was not without its eccentricities. In a Jewish precinct of New York City, Rabbi Nathan Wolf was the only voter who went to the polls. He voted for Babson and Moorman, giving them the only precinct which they carried in the country. In Missouri, the Prohibition candidate for the legislature was a clergyman actually named Santa Claus. Rev. Santa Claus received twenty-two votes.

The following year, the National Committee recommended that the next national convention consider a change in party name. They also decided for the first time that national conventions be held the year before the presidential election. This would facilitate meeting the increasingly difficult ballot laws. This tradition of meeting a full year before the presidential elections has continued down to the present day.

The year 1941 saw a rather unusual honor given to a Prohibitionist. A vacancy occurred in the United States Senate from Texas. Several of Texas' most colorful politicians entered a special election to fill the vacancy, including Sam Morris, Martin Dies, Lyndon B. Johnson and "Pappy" O'Daniel. Governor O'Daniel sought to appoint some neutral figure to serve for a few months until the special election could fill the vacancy. He decided to undercut Sam Morris' hope to use a Senate seat as a springboard for a third-party presidential bid in conjunction with the Prohibition Party. At the same time, O'Daniel hoped to win with "dry" votes himself. He appointed Andrew J. Houston, son of Sam Houston and the Prohibition candidate for governor on two occasions. At eighty-seven, Andrew J. Houston was the oldest man ever to enter the Senate for the first time. The strategy worked. Governor O'Daniel captured the Senate seat in the election.

Michigan Prohibitionists continued to gain strength as the 1942 campaign approached. Frederic S. Goodrich, former president of Albion College, ran for governor. Andrew Asikainen waged a vigorous Congressional fight. Asikainen was manager of Lansing Machining Company, involved in war production. Earlier, Asikanen had patented an invention for playgroud equipment and had operated his own production plant in this field. In the election, one county official was elected in Barry County, Michigan on the Prohibition ticket. Three more local officials were elected in Miltonvale, Kansas.

The Michigan platform adopted a broad program of social reform, urging that social concerns not be neglected in spite of the war. They urged the continuation of civil liberties in wartime. They did not mention the Japanese by name, but called for "avoidance of injustice to loyal aliens and citizens of foreign descent. . ." Heavy taxes on war profits were advocated. The widespread sale of cigarettes to the young in violation of state law was condemned.

The Arizona candidate for governor had been chairman of the state Board of Control and Commission of State Institutions. He was also a teacher of radio Bible courses. The Massachusetts candidate for State Treasurer was Martha E. Geer. Her husband, Philip W. C. Geer, was also prominent in many party activities.

Geer began as an editor and publisher of several local papers in Oregon. After working as a feature writer for the **New York Evening Mail,** he became a lecturer for the New York Academy of Sciences and the Audubon Society. A noted zoologist, he was particularly noted for his studies of the Arabian horse. He became famous for his animal sounds under the stage name of Will Cary. He produced the first cricket chirps and night sounds ever to be used in Broadway plays. He made the bird, animal and insect sounds for the famous play, **Our Town.** In addition, he played five of the different character roles in the play, performed in America and England. Philip Geer appeared as Will Cary in many plays, movies and radio programs.

The Geers and other party leaders were involved in an exciting struggle to save the Massachusetts party from infiltration in 1942. William H. McMasters, chairman of the National Pension Committee, set out to get control of the state convention and secure the gubernatorial nomination. McMasters conducted his own caucuses, but the credentials committee refused to seat his delegates. Thereupon, they held their own convention and two Prohibition slates were named. The state Ballot Law Commission ruled in favor of the regular party organization, however.

CHAPTER IX

OVER THE PEAK AND DOWN, 1944-1952

Delegates gathering in Indianapolis for the national convention in November of 1943 were cheered by the news that three Prohibitionists had just been elected to local offices in Cherrytree Township, Pennsylvania. Owing to wartime travel restrictions, only 226 delegates were able to come. Indiana had seventy delegates, each with a half vote. Twenty-seven states and the District of Columbia were represented. The National Youth Prohibition Committee continued to show vigor. There were 233 of them present.

The question of a change in name was brought up. William Varney delivered a strong address in favor of a change, but he received little support. No action was taken and the matter was not seriously considered again for many years.

The platform was longer and more specific once again. Concern was expressed for the growing power of the executive branch during wartime. Court review of the decisions of governmental departments was called for. More criticism, not less, was called for in wartime, and the platform pledged protection of diminishing states' rights. At the same time, it called for an end to racial discrimination.

The party urged a one per cent limit on all state property taxes, called for the extension of Social Security to cover everyone, and suggested several measures to prevent labor racketeering. It further advocated government programs for a smoother transition to a peace-time economy, such as job training. They endorsed membership in a world association such as the United Nations, but opposed any post-war military alliances.

Several states came to the convention pledged to Roger W. Babson, while others had been instructed to vote for Claude A. Watson. When Babson indicated that he was not interested in the nomination, the anti-Watson forces supported Sam Morris of Texas.

Watson won the nomination for president, 131-31. Sam Morris was nominated for vice president, but declined. Watson then offered to withdraw, if Morris would agree to run for president. Again Morris declined. The convention thereupon named Floyd C. Carrier of Maryland for vice president, with 130½ votes to 17½ votes for Andrew Johnson of Kentucky.

Carrier was general secretary of the American Temperance Society of the Seventh Day Adventists. Later, Carrier was disabled by a lung disease and forced to withdraw. Andrew Johnson was named in his place. Johnson was a Methodist evangelist and a widely-known lecturer on various subjects.

Indiana named a strong state ticket, with Carl W. Thompson for United States Senator. Thompson had been Randolf County prosecuting atternoy and Winchester mayor and city judge. The candidate for governor, Waldo E. Yeater, was editor of the **Farmers Exchange.** The Illinois candidate was Willis R. Wilson, president of Chicago Evangelistic Institute's board of trustees.

State conventions were quite active. The Indiana state convention drew 125 delegates. The New Jersey platform endorsed compulsory voting machines for the entire state. In Kentucky, non-partisan commissions for state institutions, higher old-age pensions, and all-weather highways were among the issues voiced at their convention.

There was active campaigning by both Watson and Johnson. Polls indicated that a large minority of the voters was in favor of wartime prohibition. Watson decided to make this his key campaign issue. Claude Watson received extensive publicity by asking for priority in air travel for presidential candidates, pointing out the wide travel privileges of the Roosevelt family. When Secretary of War Stimson refused to give him a permit for air travel, Watson called a press conference and announced that the President was afraid to take on the Prohibition Party in an open campaign. Newsmen carried the matter to a Roosevelt press conference immediately thereafter. The President turned to his assistant and asked who "this —— character" Watson was. When told, he ordered his assistant to grant Watson the permission in front of the amused reporters.

Watson travelled well over 55,000 miles in thirty-two states, much of it by air. Watson and Johnson won 74,758 votes in twenty-seven states reporting returns.

Between 1944 and 1948 a host of new personalities were attracted to party activities. In Massachusetts, Joseph T. Zottoli, Boston municipal judge, revealed startling evidence as chairman of the Massachusetts Commission to Investigate Drunkenness. Judge Zottoli's findings revealed just how much worse conditions had become since repeal, when compared with conditions before. In 1945, he appeared before the annual conference of state Prohibitionists to expound on his findings. Although he was always persistent in refusing to run for office on the state ticket, he remained an unofficial party sympathizer. He spoke at the 1948 state convention and various party functions thereafter.

While baseball evangelist Billy Sunday had never felt that he should openly endorse the Prohibition Party, his heirs became far more active in party affairs. Ma Sunday became particularly prominent at party gatherings. Homer Rodeheaver, trombonist and lead musician of the Sunday crusades over the years, also took part. He composed the hymns, "Then Jesus Came," and "You Must Open the Door," among others. As owner of a leading fundamentalist music publishing corporation, he arranged a strategy session between Babson and fundamentalist church leaders in the 1940 campaign. At that time, he envisioned the fundamentalists as the wave of the future as old-line Protestant churches became more liberal. He also saw the party as a means of exerting this social and political influence. In the late 1940's, Rodeheaver went to work building the party's youth organization by holding rallies. Another attraction at these meetings was his associate, Bentley D. Ackley. Composer of some 2,000 songs, Ackley was best known for such hymns as "Mother's Prayers Have Followed Me," "God Understands," "In the Service of the King," "I Want to Be There at the Roll-Call," "Transformed," "Let the Beauty of Jesus Be Seen in Me," "I Would Be Like Jesus," "Joy in Serving Jesus," and "If Your Heart Keeps Right." The party's poet laureate during the period was Judge Frank E. Herrick of Wheaton, Illinois. His poems were printed or set to music as propaganda material in many partisan campaigns.

The 1946 mid-term elections attracted some interesting figures in the California races. A former Congressman, John H. Hoeppel, ran on the

Prohibition ticket for Congress. The party also enlisted handsome, 39-year-old Douglas Corrigan to run for the United States Senate. A mechanic and flying instructor, he had been one of the workmen on the "Spirit of St. Louis." An admirer of Charles Lindberg, he became a pioneer aviator in his own right. In 1938, he made a non-stop flight from California to New York. His plane was nine years old, with a single engine, no radio, and without adequate flying instruments. Taking off for the return trip to California, he flew over the Atlantic instead, landing in Dublin, Ireland. Always shy and modest, he refused to claim that he had flown there deliberately. The press dubbed him "Wrong Way" Corrigan and his autobiography, **This Is My Story,** became widely read. Even before his California campaign, he had developed a good deal of speaking experience in war rallies in movie theaters around the country.

One of the Iowa candidates was president of Boone Bible College. In Illinois, the ticket included the president of Greenville College and the former dean of Moody Bible Institute. Virginia's candidate for the United States Senate, Thomas E. Boorde, was president of General Welfare Foundation of America. This group worked for the liberalization of Social Security.

The Indiana state convention drew well over 500 delegates, and county tickets were named in fifty-four counties. The party's youth organization tried using the old Venango Plan in several of these county contests. However, county newspapers reported on the eve of the elections that the youth had failed to get enough pledges to carry the county. Even though this was not true in some instances, many who had pledged to vote for the ticket felt that they were released from the pledge. In spite of this, the party polled about 25% of the vote in those counties where the Venango Plan was used.

In one Virginia Congressional district the party polled 13% of the vote. In Jewell County, Kansas, three Prohibitionists were elected in Walnut Township and the candidate for sheriff was nearly elected. In Roxbury, New Hampshire, the state chairman was able to elect the state legislator for that town by the write-in method.

The national convention assembled in June of 1947 in Billy Sunday Tabernacle at Winona Lake, Indiana. There were 301 delegates and 77 alternates from twenty-nine states and the District of Columbia. One of the evening rallies drew more than 2,500 people. A small group pressed to bring up the question of a name change, but the opposition was stronger than ever.

Nominations for president were made for Dr. Colvin, Claude Watson and Dr. Enoch A. Holtwick. Colvin withdrew and threw his support to Holtwick, developing a spirited contest. Dr. Holtwick had been president of Los Angeles Pacific Junior College, before returning to Illinois to head the history department at Greenville College. The California delegation backed him, in spite of it being Watson's home state. Watson, however, was renominated, 150-117.

An effort was made to name a woman for vice president. Mamie Colvin and Ethel Hubler, editor of the **National Voice,** were nominated. However, they both declined and the convention turned to Dale H. Learn of Pennsylvania. Learn was a prominent businessman who had been president of the Pennsylvania Real Estate Association and president of the Monroe County Insurance Association. He was trustee and alumni president of East Stroudsburg State Teachers College. He was an officer in many civic and religious organizations, such as president of the Lehigh Valley Layman's Association.

The platform was much the same as the previous one with a few exceptions. It called for international inspection and control of atomic energy. It further expressed opposition to peacetime conscription as a bad influence on the morals of youth and a potential threat of military entrenchment in the government. The platform urged a government program to alleviate the housing shortage, but generally it opposed high taxes and government spending.

Once again the party enjoyed the support of many religious leaders. The Ohio gubernatorial candidate was John C. Williams, but death removed him from the race. Williams had been president of Westminster College in Texas and chancellor of Kansas City University. Among Indiana campaigners were Dr. F. W. Lough and Dr. J. A. Huffman. Lough was national superintendent of the Clean Life League. Huffman was a leading Mennonite Bible scholar who had engaged in excavations of the Holy Land. He has since been a contributor to the **Higley Commentary** and the author of two books on the Revised Standard Version of the Bible. For many years, he edited the **Gospel Banner** and was founding president of the World-Wide Bible-Readers Fellowship. In higher education, he was dean of Taylor University's School of Religion. Later, he was president of Bethel College and dean of the Winona Lake School of Theology in the summers. He served the Prohibition Party for many years as treasurer.

The candidate for lieutenant governor on the Michigan ticket had been the two-term president of the American Millers' Association. He was also an associate of Henry Ford in carrying out the "Lord's Acre" project. A film financed by Ford had widely publicized his experience in tithing a piece of land by setting aside the produce of it for church work. In Oregon, Paul F. Petticord took a leading part in the campaign. President of Western School of Evangelical Religion, he was district superintendent of the Evangelical United Brethren. He was aided by Dr. C. J. Pike, president of Cascade College.

If the party's campaigns during this period did nothing else, they did provide a means to publicize many new and struggling fundamentalist schools. In this way, the party played an important role in consolidating and institutionalizing this religious movement. Only in the Prohibition Party did the fundamentalist splinter groups have a common meeting ground with the nineteenth-century liberals who had been trained at colleges which had once had a Christian emphasis. The relationship between the two was always an uneasy one, but a beneficial one all the same.

In Pennsylvania, Dr. R. R. Blews, eminent historian and Bible scholar, became state chairman. Blews had been president of Evansville Junior College in Wisconsin and later dean of Greenville College. But no list of party crusaders of this period would be complete without mention of J. Raymond Schmidt. Schmidt, editor of several reform periodicals, was prominent for many years in leading the temperance lobby in Washington, D.C.

Claude Watson's colorful style of campaigning pushed the Prohibition Party to its highest vote since the enactment of prohibition. Between elections, Watson had learned to fly with much fanfare. At the opening of the 1948 campaign, he purchased a new, four-passenger, single-engine plane in which he barnstormed the country. He gained added publicity by sending his wife on a tour of the White House. She then released to the press a list of alterations that she would make when her husband became its chief resident.

The number of states on the ballot dropped back to nineteen. In spite of this setback, the vote for Watson and Learn continued to soar. They received 103,343 votes.

The 1950 mid-term elections produced some interesting incidents. In the Kansas Prohibition primary, there was a contest for the gubernatorial nomination. The winner was C. Floyd Hester, who had done extensive YMCA work in northern China. He had been principal of Friends Academy, as well as president of Wesleyan Methodist College. After both of the World Wars, he did extensive work around the country for European relief. During the campaign, he was particularly active in building up local tickets. As a result, nineteen Prohibitionists were elected in six Kansas towns, and yet another missed election by two votes. Four of the towns were in Hester's own Jewell County.

Four local officials were also elected in Heth Township of Harrison County, Indiana. The Massachusetts candidate for Auditor was a Negro dentist. Several Negroes were active in the party from that state over the years. In a special election for Los Angeles County district attorney, Claude Watson polled 322,422 votes.

As the 1952 campaign approached, several new religious leaders loaned their support to the party. Ma Sunday kicked off the drive for funds with the first contribution. Dr. Leroy Lowell, director of the nationally-known broadcast "Light and Life Hour," agreed to run for the United States Senate in Michigan. Mr. and Mrs. Virgil Brock, both widely known hymn-writers, also helped the party in many ways. The Brocks are best known for their hymns, "Beyond the Sunset," "He's a Wonderful Savior to Me," and the children's chorus, "Sing and Smile and Pray."

Most active among the new adherents was Bishop Wilbur E. Hammaker of Washington, D.C. Originally a missionary bishop in China, Hammaker returned after the trouble with Japan. He was a leader in the America First Committee and was chairman of the Citizens' Unemployment Relief Committee. After retirement as bishop of the Denver area, he served in Washington as president of three important temperance organizations. He edited **Progress Magazine** and was a major leader of the anti-liquor lobby in the nation's capital.

The 1951 national convention in Indianapolis was electrified by the news that Stuart Hamblen had agreed to take part in the proceedings. Hamblen had been a cowboy singer for twenty-one years on a Warner Brothers radio show. Both he and his wife were composers of folk songs and religious music. A convert of Billy Graham, Hamblen had starred in such popular Graham films as "Oil City, U.S.A." Turning to religious music, he wrote, "It Is No Secret What God Can Do," the first gospel song ever to reach the Hit Parade. His early cowboy song of greatest fame was "Open Up Your Heart and Let the Sunshine In." His religious songs were such ones as "Beside Still Waters," "Your Must Be Born Again," "I Believe," and "How Big Is God."

The pre-convention rally at Indianapolis drew 5,000 people to hear Stuart Hamblen. The next day, he flew on to New York for recordings, while the convention debated whether to nominate him for president.

Party regulars warned that the party had suffered at the hands of newcomers in the past. Led by William Varney, they presented Enoch Holtwick as their choice. Once again, the California delegation backed him against a candidate from their own state.

At the end of the nominating speech for Hamblen, some time was yielded to the convention song-leader, who sang, "It Is No Secret." When the vote was taken, Hamblen won, 74-41. The convention was swept by a large demonstration, as delegates marched about the hall, singing the Hit Parade gospel song which soon became the campaign theme. Holtwick was nominated for vice president.

The platform revealed the growing conservatism of the party. Socialistic trends in the government were condemned. The party charged that Social Secuilty funds were being misused. Referring to the findings of the Kefauver Crime Committee, they condemned the hold that organized crime exerted over the major parties. The evil of Communism and the danger of subversive infiltration were also proclaimed.

The students at Purdue University were the first to launch a Hamblen-for-President Club, and the movement soon spread. The four radio and television networks donated fifteen minutes of time to him. The 1952 summer conference in the Billy Sunday Tabernacle drew 6,000 people to hear him. During Hamblen's tour of the Midwest alone, his rallies drew 20,000 listeners, not to mention many radio and television appearances.

Hamblen and Holtwick were on the ballot in twenty states, as it was growing increasingly difficult to meet the ever more stringent requirements. A particularly hard loss was that of the Illinois ballot. But in the 1952 election, a sheriff and thirteen other local officials were elected in Jewell County, Kansas. Hamblen and Holtwick polled 78,818 votes.

CHAPTER X

HOLDING ON AFTER THE DELUGE, 1952-1962

The 1954 elections marked the beginning of a series of setbacks for the party. For the first time since the founding of the party, Pennsylvania lost its place on the ballot, never regained because of more stringent laws. The entire Massachusetts ticket was also ruled off the ballot on a legal technicality.

The Massachusetts organization had drafted a liberal platform, praising the value of neutrality of India and opposing an American military alliance with them. They called for revision of the McCarren-Walter Act and urged the admission of 240,000 displaced persons to this country. They praised United Nations relief efforts.

Indiana and Michigan lost their automatic place on the ballot due to a moderate decline in their showing. However, Kansas and California continued to show strength. The sheriff of Jewell County was re-elected. The Kansas candidate for lieutenant governor won nearly 40,000 votes. The candidate for attorney general of California, Edwin M. Cooper, won 204,000 votes. Cooper, a prominent attorney, had administered fifteen million dollars in social services as a Y.M.C.A. and U.S.O. executive.

Three disastrous events contributed to the decline of the Prohibition Party. Before they had run their course, the party had been demoralized to the point of near extinction. The party's drift toward the Right alienated many members of its active youth organization. Extreme leftists in the movement decided to form their own organization, Democracy Unlimited. E. Harold Munn, Jr., manager of two Michigan radio stations, tried to carry on with those who remained. However, the Young Prohibitionists Association was demoralized.

The second crisis was a financial one. Dr. Gerald Overholt had become national chairman prior to the 1952 campaign. When he took office, the party was nearly $5,000 in debt. Overholt launched a vigorous campaign, sending many speakers across the country. A good deal of money was raised, particularly with the help of Stuart Hamblen. But much more was spent. By 1953, the party debt had accumulated to over $20,000 and Overholt resigned as chairman. Some $70,000 had been spent in the 1952 campaign alone.

The third problem was created by his successor as chairman, Dr. Lowell H. Coate. Dr. Coate was a long-time party worker, but he had developed associations which would soon create problems. He was a sociologist and supervisor of the Child Welfare Department of the Los Angeles Board of Education. He had also founded Pacific International Univesity, which pioneered in adult education. A native of Indiana, he was president of the Hoosier State Society in California.

Dr. Coate had long been involved in the peace movement. He had co-authored the last book written by William Jennings Bryan, **The Dawn of Humanity.** For twelve years, he was president of the Foreign Policy Council of Los Angeles. The State Department appointed him as a special delegate to the 1948 UNESCO Conference.

One of the men whom Coate began to groom was Brigadier General Herbert C. Holdridge, the "Peace General" from California. An Eisenhower classmate at West Point and a Pentagon administrator, the general had been forced into retirement because of the Holdridge Plan. His proposal was to create a fourth branch of the government to direct the economy. He reasoned that capitalism was doomed. After an attempt to form a party of his own to promote the plan, he became the presidential candidate of the virtually non-existent Vegetarian Party in 1952. Later, he was initiated into the Mohawk tribe and became leader of the American Indian nationalistic movement, demanding the return of America to their control. Among his several peculiar associations, his daughter appeared nightly as a "Mousekateer" on the television show of Walt Disney's Mickey Mouse Club.

Prohibitionists were kept unaware of these associations, but they could read his militantly anti-Catholic articles which Coate began to print in the party's newspaper. When several party leaders asked Coate to resign, he insisted that he would stay on until the 1955 convention. He dealt with all these disagreements far more openly on the pages of the **National Prohibitionist** than anyone had previously.

Dr. Coate selected Camp Mack, north of Winona Lake headquarters, as the site of the 1955 national convention. The date was chosen to coincide with the closing of a conference of the Fellowship of Reconciliation at the same place. Coate planned to have many of these pacifists remain as delegates to take control of the Prohibition national convention. This hope proved false, however. In addition, he laid plans to have two bus-loads of leftists come in from Chicago to outvote party regulars. Perhaps these were members of the dissident Democracy Unlimited.

He planned to have them change the party's name. To lay the groundwork, he emphasized the party's declining electoral strength and the need to broaden its horizons. A resolution favorable to the change was passed by the Kansas state committee, and Dr. F. W. Lough also wrote an article supporting the idea.

Dr. Coate proposed Republican Senator William Langer of North Dakota as the standard-bearer. Langer was acceptable to Prohibitionists because he had sponsored a bill in Congress to prohibit liquor advertising over the mass media. To the Coate faction of socialist or pacifist bent, Langer had Populist-styled origins in the Non-Partisan League. At the same time, he was an isolationist in foreign affairs, which was viewed favorably by the pacifists. He was presented to Prohibitionists as a man who had experience in many governmental posts, including state attorney general and governor of North Dakota before entering the United States Senate.

Senator Langer agreed to come to the Prohibition national convention to speak. He was received by an audience of about 300 people. Listeners noted that he spent considerable time in his address going over his credentials as though he were looking for a nomination. Meantime, the credentials committee refused to seat delegates who would not pledge loyalty to the Prohibition Party. Since many of Coate's associates were outsiders who would not make such a pledge, it was decided to hold a rump convention in the evening before the regular convention convened. The name was changed to American Pioneers Party and William Langer was nominated for president. Prohibition Party leaders were aroused in the middle of the night, party records and offices were locked up, and the press was told that the action was not that of the party's convention.

But there was still General Holdridge of California. Most party leaders were favorably impressed with his appearance at the convention since they were unaware of his radical associations. William Varney once again fought for the cause of Enoch Holtwick and warned the party of its past misfortunes with newcomers and opportunists. A young newcomer, Earl F. Dodge of Massachusetts ,agreed with him, however. Dodge was aware of Holdridge's background and joined Varney in seeking to get Holtwick nominated.

The key was the Indiana delegation which controlled nearly a third of the convention votes. The state leaders supported Holdridge. But when the vote came, more than two-thirds of the delegates heeded Dodge's lobbying by supporting Holtwick. He was narrowly nominated, 56-51. There had originally been 154 delegates from sixteen states and the District of Columbia.

General Holdridge was nominated for vice president and he did important work in California to keep the party on the ballot there. Prohibitionists needed more registrations to maintain the party primary there. Party workers pushed the enrollment up to 5,420, many more than the required number. Holdridge, however, began to make demands on the party which it could not meet. He withdrew and was replaced by Edwin M. Cooper of California, who had made such a good showing in the 1951 elections.

The 1956 platform of Holtwick and Cooper called for more economic aid for needy peoples of the world. Co-operatives and profit-sharing were endorsed as usual. Price support programs for the farmers were condemned. The party called for direct election of the president and vice president, home rule and Congressional representation for the District of Columbia, statehood for Alaska and Hawaii, full citizenship for Indians, and encouragement of self-rule for Puerto Rico, the Virgin Islands, Guam and Samoa.

The discouraging events of recent years dampened the campaign. Nevertheless, CBS and ABC networks gave Holtwick and Cooper a half-hour of evening television time, and CBS radio also carried the broadcast. The number of states on the ballot was cut in half (down to ten). However, the vote in those states compared favorably to 1952. Holtwick and Cooper won 41,937 votes.

In state contests, Earl F. Dodge won 10,030 votes for Secretary of State in Massachusetts. The Kansas United Dry Forces endorsed H. O. Lytle for governor. A five-car caravan waged a 700-mile campaign tour of the state. Lytle was credited with 20,894 votes, despite the usual "count-out" of minor party votes. It was the largest vote that any party candidate at the top of the state ticket had ever received in Kansas. Jewell County's sheriff was elected County Treasurer and eight other Prohibitionists were elected there.

The party held its own in the 1958 mid-term elections. Massachusetts called for an end to further nuclear testing and its top vote-getter received 8,300 ballots. The highest state-wide totals in other states were: Kansas, 28,713; Indiana, 19,327; and California, nearly 130,000. Special efforts were also made to revive the organization in New Hampshire and Rhode Island.

The following year, there was a special election for Supreme Court Justice in Michigan. Although the candidates were not listed by party on the ballot, political parties named and endorsed the candidates. The

Prohibition candidate received 199,123 votes (22%). A slate was also entered in the municipal elections at Winona Lake, Indiana. The party captured control of the Town Board by winning two out of three seats. Norman Bradfield became chairman of the board. The other Prohibitionist was Virgil Brock.

Meanwhile in Kansas, a Democratic governor preferred appointing Prohibitionists to naming Republicans. He was required to appoint at least two out of five members on bi-partisan commissions from outside of his own party. He named two Prohibitionists, Warren C. Martin and Harry O. Lytle, to the Kansas State Board of Paroles and Pardons. Lytle served a term as chairman.

Two years later, a similar situation developed on the Hagertown, Indiana, school board. Required to be bi-partisan, a deadlock developed over which party should have the deciding vote. They decided to name a Prohibitionist, Horace Smith, a Quaker farm manager. When the regular elections were held, Smith entered the race and polled about twice as many votes as any of the other candidates of either major party. He was also elected board secretary at the organizational meeting. Other Prohibitionists also held local offices in other states, especially in Maine.

The national convention of 1959 met in Winona Lake, Indiana. A special meaning was added to it by the fact that it was the party's ninetieth anniversary. Virgil Brock wrote two special anniversary songs for the occasion. The better liked of the two was "I'd Rather Be Right." There were 165 delegates and alternates, with a nearly equal number of visitors.

The convention chose Dr. Rutherford L. Decker for the presidential nomination. Dr. Decker had been president of the Colorado Baptist Convention and the Rocky Mountain Bible Conference. He was founder of the Denver Rescue Mission and the Colorado School of the Bible. He moved to Kansas City, Missouri, to become pastor of the 1,200-member Temple Baptist Church. At this inner-city church, Dr. Decker carried on an active program for the poor without government aid. He became president of the Kansas-Missouri Baptist Welfare Association and founded the Temple Foundation which provided housing for the aged. Dr. Decker was so active in fighting the notorious political machine in Kansas City that his church was bombed and burned in 1948.

Decker was one of the founders of the National Association of Evangelicals, chief rival of the National Council of Churches. He was an early president of the N.A.E. For many years, he also served as its executive secretary.

The vice presidential choice went to E. Harold Munn, Sr., who had spent most of his career in college teaching. At Greenville College, Munn had been acting dean and registrar. At the time of his nomination, he was associate dean at Hillsdale College in charge of the college's teacher-training program. Mr. Munn was a major share-holder in several radio and television stations, being president of Twin Valley Broadcasters, Inc.

The platform of Decker and Munn continued the conservative trend of the party. It urged a gradual return to the gold standard, the sale of government businesses to private owners, the application of anti-trust laws to labor unions. The delegates endorsed right-to-work laws and urged that secondary boycotts and industry-wide bargaining be made illegal. They condemned foreign aid to any undemocratic nation, and opposed federal aid to education. As usual, they opposed the use of public funds to aid religious schools in any way, but they favored continued tax exemption for non-profit religious enterprises. There was also the usual endorsement of racial equality, but racial violence on both sides was condemned.

Efforts were made to secure a place on many more state ballots. However, the party found the legal requirements increasingly difficult to meet. Decker and Munn were on the ballot in only eleven states. At the 1960 Democratic National Convention in Los Angeles, California Prohibitionists picketed for their candidate. This drew mention in the first of Theodore White's now famous series of political analyses (**The Making of the President, 1960).**

Party loyalists were subjected to pressure and even to persecution by Protestant extremists, owing to the fact that the Democratic candidate was a Roman Catholic. In California, the Decker campaign made excellent progress. In the closing days, Republican leaders saw that the vote in California would be close. They spread the word among Prohibitionists that Decker had withdrawn in favor of Nixon, and many clergymen in Prohibition strongholds announced it from the pulpits before election day.

In spite of the difficulties, the vote in California nearly doubled over the previous presidential election (to 21,706). Had it not been for this, the vote nationally would have revealed a decline due to many desertions in the states where the fundamentalist vote was important. In the South, however, there were gains. Tennessee and Alabama reported the largest votes since the turn of the century. Record votes were polled in Texas and New Mexico. But the national ticket had never been strong historically in the South anyway. The total for Decker and Munn was 46,239 votes from eleven states.

In a Navajo precinct near Shiprock, New Mexico, most of the voters were illiterates who customarily voted a straight Democratic ticket. When the Democratic place on the ballot was changed to second place from its customary place at the top, party leaders worked hard to get the voters to pull the bottom lever instead of the top one. What they forgot was that Decker's ticket was third on the voting machine. When the votes were counted, Decker polled 177 votes out of some two hundred votes cast. It was the one precinct in the country that was carried by the Prohibition ticket, compensating in a small way for the many legitimate votes that were never counted. National news commentators also had a few chuckles over the party's presidential elector in Montana, Harry A. Boozer.

CHAPTER XI

EVENTS AND PROSPECTS OF THE PAST DECADE, 1962-1972

The 1962 mid-term elections brought mixed results. Michigan failed to gain the ballot for the first time since the founding of the party. The loss would prove to be lasting as the new restrictions were imposed by a change in the law. Part of the problem was created by the decision of the state committee (by a vote of five to four) to change the name to the American Christian Party. The new name brought little response from outsiders, while creating suspicion among party regulars. Later, the national party conducted a referendum on the proposal of a change in name. Party members defeated it by a two-thirds vote. The margin in Michigan, where the experiment had been tried twice, was about 75% opposed. The party did play one important role in Michigan in spite of the loss of a place on the ballot. The party supported the new state constitution. Since it was adopted by a razor-thin margin, the party's support of it was probably vital.

During the 1962 campaign the party's paper called for a blockade of Cuba, when it became clear that Russian missiles were being installed there. The Prohibitionists were the first party to call for such action, later taken by the President. In Massachusetts a Worcester physician, with considerable cooperation from the city's Roman Catholic hierarchy, waged a vigorous campaign for Congress. He polled over 15,000 votes. There were about 8,000 additional votes cast elsewhere in the state for the general ticket. The candidate for auditor in Kansas, Rolland E. Fisher, polled over 62,000 votes, or about 13% of the total. Two state-wide California candidates polled 120,000 and 115,000 votes respectively. The larger figure was barely the 2% required to remain on the ballot.

For several years, a vigorous Prohibition ticket had been entered in Lake County, Indiana. This county included the cities of Gary and East Chicago, and both major parties had become notoriously corrupt. In 1962, a slate of forty-five candidates was filed. Lake County Prohibitionists played an important role in stirring public reaction against a corrupt, bi-partisan political machine. It was not long afterwards that a considerable reform movement made an impact on the city government of Gary. A similar situation occurred in Massachusetts where the party captured the balance of power in the governor's race. The winning candidate moved to crack down on illegal gambling and sought to abolish the death penalty, two issues on which the Prohibition candidate had campaigned.

The 1963 national convention was held in St. Louis. By choosing to meet in a metropolitan area, the party received far more attention in the mass media than for many years. There were seventy-two delegates from nineteen states and the District of Columbia, with about one hundred visitors. Special honors were given to Fred Squires, one of the original founders of the American Businessmen's Research Foundation in Chicago. This organization had made many important statistical studies over the years, particularly on the liquor problem. Several of its leaders have been affiliated with the party. The convention was especially pleased by a party endorsement delivered in person by Mrs. Fred J. Tooze, president of the National WCTU.

A spirited contest developed over the presidential nomination. The candidate of those in control of the convention was E. Harold Munn, Sr. However, a strong effort was made in behalf of Milton C. Conover, a New Jersey law professor. While on the Yale faculty in 1932, Conover had led the Connecticut Independent Republican movement mentioned earlier. A change of two votes would have given Conover the presidential nomination.

Munn was nominated for president and Conover for vice president. However, when Conover declined, the convention turned to Rev. Mark R. Shaw. A Methodist clergyman, Shaw was one of the party's most widely travelled members. He had worked in temperance and peace groups in several parts of the world. A central figure in the party's liberal, internationalist wing, he was particularly prominent in the Fellowship of Reconciliation. He had been the key figure in the Massachusetts organization for many years.

The platform was nearly the same as that of 1960. A voluntary system of Social Security was added to the planks. Furthermore, the Supreme Court was condemned in stronger terms for acting as a legislative body, particularly in the ban on prayer and Bible-reading in public schools.

The most serious blow to the Munn-Shaw campaign was in California. The state chairman, Robert Wyckoff, both a physician and a lawyer, was alienating the party faithful by his far-rightist activities. He began to advocate that Senator Goldwater's name appear at the top of the Prohibition ticket. The crucial need was to keep up the party's registration so that it could hold primary elections. Wyckoff's activities did not persuade right-wing Republicans to register as Prohibitionists. Indeed, he even sabotaged such efforts. At the same time, regular partisans lost their enthusiasm for soliciting new registrations. As a result, the party was ruled off the ballot for the first time since the Populist era. California had become increasingly the cornerstone of electoral support, but the state law made it impossible to regain the ballot once it was lost.

The party also failed to gain the ballot in Michigan in spite of great effort. The ballot was won in only nine states. Of these, only Indiana had a tradition of giving the national ticket a large vote. For the first time in the party's history, however, extensive write-in campaigns were waged with measureable success in Michigan and California.

The most important speech of the campaign was delivered to the student body at Kansas State University by Mr. Munn. One of his more colorful experiences was a Sunday tour of several Negro churches in New York and a speech in Central Park. A Republican paper with anti-Goldwater sentiments wrote an article which came very close to endorsing him. But all this could produce little results since the party could not meet the state's ballot law requirements. Returns from eleven states gave Munn and Shaw 23,267 votes. In addition, there was a "scattering" of write-ins; 5,429 in California, 1,313 in Connecticut, 2,509 in Oregon, and 2,531 in Pennsylvania. A large portion of these were Prohibition votes.

One of the Kansas state candidates polled more than 18,000 votes (13,000 more than the national ticket received there). A Massachusetts candidate captured nearly 12,000 votes, three times that of the national ticket in that state. Both Massachusetts tallies were the largest that the party had received there in decades. The Massachusetts presidenial vote was, in fact, the highest in half a century.

Dr. D. D. Gibbons, the national chairman, was active in getting better legal standing for minor parties. He had to carry one case to the Michigan Supreme Court, in order to gain the right to have write-in votes counted. Another case was carried to the United States Supreme Court, challenging the harrassment of minor parties by increasingly difficult ballot laws. The Supreme Court, however, refused to even hear the case.

Another of Dr. Gibbons' achievements was the launching of the Temperance Education Crusade. Through this emphasis, he was able to persuade party representatives in several states to carry on temperance programs in the public schools and Sunday schools. There are several such programs now in operation which the party has encouraged over the years. Dr. Gibbons himself was particularly successful with his talking robot, Tommy Tune-O-Meter.

The 1966 party conference in Kansas City called for an end to the "War on Poverty." It endorsed the Dirksen Amendment to restore prayer and Bible-reading to the public schools. For the first time in many years, Iowa had a state ticket in a mid-term election. Their vote doubled over 1964.

The 1967 national convention met in Detroit. There were seventy delegates with forty-eight convention votes. Fourteen states and the District of Columbia were represented. E. Harold Munn was again placed before the convention for the presidential nomination, along with several favorite son candidates. Those opposing a second nomination for Munn chiefly supported Mark Shaw of Massachusetts. Munn was nominated on the second ballot. Rolland E. Fisher, a Free Methodist evangelist from Topeka, Kansas, was chosen for vice president.

The platform urged the federal government to adopt a tax-sharing program with the states through use of the income tax. The heavily graduated nature of the income tax was condemned, however. Foreign aid should largely be in the form of "repayable loans," the platform stated. Defending the principle of neighborhood schools, it expressed opposition to artificial integration by busing.

The party upheld the concept of national sovereignty and opposed surrender of it to any international group. Peacetime national defense should be left to "professionally trained volunteers." Programs of "mass medication" such as floridation of water were opposed. In mental health programs, the platform warned against "unjust and prejudiced incarcerations."

The most important meeting of the 1968 campaign was a televized presentation by Munn at New York University. It was broadcast nationwide on National Educational Television. However, regular television networks continued their trend of giving less and less coverage to minor party efforts. In Michigan, enough signatures were submitted for state requirements for the first time. But there were enough that were ruled off by state officials to prevent the party from having a place on the ballot again. In New Mexico, the required state convention was held, but state officials waited until the deadline to notify the party that a technical error had been made in filing the papers. Thus, the party was able to meet the requirements in only nine states, although write-in efforts were made in three others.

The vote fell off disastrously in 1968. The vote in Indiana was only half of what it had been in 1964. Even in several other states where the presidential vote is usually less crucial to a good showing, the returns were only a fraction of what they had been. On the other hand, the vote in Massachusetts was the second highest since 1916. For the first time since 1944, a ticket was fielded in Virginia with fair results. Nevertheless, had it not been for a record vote in Alabama (4,022), the results would have looked even worse than they did. The total from twelve states for Munn and Fisher was 15,123 votes, the lowest total since the 1880 campaign of Neal Dow. Five candidates for state office in Kansas polled several thousand more votes than the party's entire national total. The candidate for state treasurer polled 21,361 votes.

On September 1 and 2 of 1969, ninety-five of the party faithful from twelve states met in Detroit to celebrate the 100th anniversary of the Prohibition Party. No other minor party in American history had reached such a milestone. But the press gave the event virtually no attention and only one reporter covered the sessions. There was much concern over the party's future after the 1968 showing. Yet nearly everyone expressed determination to carry on. The National Committee voted to proclaim the next year as the Centennial Year of the Prohibition Party. It also instructed its officers to begin a study of the party's future plans.

Several resolutions were endorsed. The party expressed concern over the proliferation of conglomerate business structures. Apprehension was expressed about the way sex education was being treated in many school programs. Implied consent laws in relation to drunken driving were endorsed. One resolution urged home rule for the Virgin Islands, self-government for Micronesia, and American citizenship for the people of Samoa. Acts of violence and terror to gain civil rights were condemned. The most spirited argument came over whether to condemn our public officials for fraternizing with dictators and countries practicing oppression. The motion to adopt such a resolution was carried.

After the observance was over, Prohibitionists turned their attention to a municipal election to see if the party could still hope to have any pulling power at the polls. Earl Dodge entered the non-partisan race for the Kalamazoo City Commission as a much-publicized party member. Dodge had already gained widespread support as a close associate of the city government. Kalamazoo, Michigan, a city of 90,000 had served as the party's headquarters for a number of years. Earl Dodge, the party's national Executive Secretary, had been a founder and president of the Good Government Association. As such, he was active in supporting the incumbent mayor, and the city received a citation as one of the top-ten cities in the United States. The City Commission appointed Dodge to two appointive offices. He was made a member of the Community Relations Board, which was particularly concerned with racial problems. The second position was that of the Greater Kalamazoo Council, having to do with long-ranged urban planning.

Shortly after the anniversary celebration, Earl Dodge announced that he would seek a seat on the City Commission in his own right. It was noted in the press that he was the leading officer in the Prohibition Party's national headquarters. He campaigned actively for about a month throughout the city. It was the first time that the party had sought an office in a city of that size in half a century with a chance of winning the election. When the votes were counted, Dodge polled 6,470 votes, about 2,000 less than were needed for election. It was the largest vote that the party had polled in Michigan for over a decade, even for a state-wide office.

The party found three young men to head up the state tickets in 1970. Concentrated efforts were made in Kansas, Massachusetts and Alabama. The Massachusetts platform called for the repeal of the sales tax to be replaced by the use of existing taxing methods plus a tax on pollution. A vigorous program to combat pollution was urged. Also, a better mass transit system was endorsed, including the return of publicly owned systems to private enterprise. The platform proposed a better program of educating the under-employed, including the addition of a thirteenth year of education in the public school system. It called for updating of the laws on cruelty to animals and the enforcement of laws on pornography. Among the governmental reforms proposed were: recodification of state laws, use of data processing and cost accounting, more self-rule for local governments, public referendums on urban renewal projects, reduction in the size of the state House of Representatives, and enlargement of the Executive Council.

In Alabama, the Republican Party decided to enter no state ticket in the 1970 elections. Thus, the Prohibition Party was the only group to enter a full slate of six candidates other than the two Democratic factions in Alabama. Prohibitionists looked forward to a good showing there. In addition to these larger efforts, Pennsylvania Prohibitionists have continued to run local tickets over the years, even though they have been unable to meet the ballot laws for state-wide contests. In 1966, they were able to poll enough votes in Venango County to be given full status for holding their own party primaries there.

Two local campaigns were waged in 1970 in Pennsylvania. One of those recruited to aid the effort was Lester Pendleton, sheriff of McKean County. Sheriff Pendleton addressed a party rally and accepted a position on the party's state committee. A write-in campaign was waged in California for seven candidates, although state election officials refused to count the votes received.

In Kansas, the party sparked a campaign to prevent liquor-by-the-drink in a referendum which drew nation-wide publicity. The question was defeated and party voters provided the margin of victory for its opponents. Harry O. Lytle also captured the balance of power in the race for lieutenant governor, polling 22,084 votes. More than a quarter of this (6,477) came from his home county, where he ran up seven per cent of the vote in the state's most populous county.

The state auditor's position is one of keeping watch of finances, waste and corruption in many states. Returns from the three states where the party entered a state ticket revealed that voters continued to give the Prohibition Party a high degree of trust for this office. The candidate for auditor in Kansas received 19,743 votes with four candidates for other offices polling comparable totals. In Massachusetts, the auditor candidate polled 13,373 votes with two candidates for other offices receiving somewhat smaller totals. The candidate for auditor in Alabama polled 23,024 votes. Thus the total for auditor in the three states was 56,140 votes.

Jerome B. Couch, the candidate for governor in Alabama, was the first party candidate for state office in many years to receive national publicity. In spite of the fact that there were six candidates for governor, one a Republican and two Democratic factions, Couch polled a record total of 9,705 votes. Even the percentage showings were exceeded only by the election of 1900. Candidates for Commissioner of Agriculture and Treasurer polled nearly two per cent of the vote (13,449 and 14,769 respectively). A candidate for the State Board of Education in one district polled nearly three per cent of the vote, while the candidate for Auditor polled more than three per cent.

The party continues to have some prominent supporters. Dr. C. J. Haggard, president of Azusa Pacific College in California, is one. Rollin M. Severance of Saginaw, Michigan is another erstwhile candidate and financial backer. His corporation manufactures high-quality tools that are widely known.

Dr. Andrew C. Ivy's works have been increasingly promoted by the party in recent years, and he has become a financial contributor. A world-renowned medical doctor associated with the University of Chicago, he was a World War II commander in the Aviation Medical Naval Reserve Corps. During the same period, he was president of the Chicago Institute of Medicine, the American Physiological Society, and the American Gastro-Enterological Association. He also served the last group for ten years as managing editor of their periodical. He has written two books and more than 1500 scientific articles. In recent years, he received national publicity when federal authorities prosecuted him for fraud in the promotion of a cancer cure. He was exonerated during the trial and cleared of the charges.

The Prohibition National Convention met June 24-25, 1971 at the First Church of the Nazarene in Wichita, Kansas. It was the furthest west and south that a party convention had ever been held. The number of out-of-state delegates was considerably larger than for many years. But the local attendance was much smaller than usual, owing to the distance of the convention from any base of substantial local support. Fifty-two delegates were certified from fourteen states and the District of Columbia. There were some thirty-five other observers and guests. An unusual feature was the seating of four teen-age delegates who were below the age of eighteen.

In spite of the effort of some to write the platform as a brief philosophical statement of principles, the platform was longer than usual in the final draft. Stronger statements were made against inflation, government spending, and the general state of the economy. Environmental concerns were voiced, although nuclear reactors for electricity were endorsed. It called for enforcement of laws against strikes by federal employees, and the emphasis of many leaders on civil disobedience was condemned.

The plank on church-state relations supported a continued tax-exempt status for non-profit religious enterprises and property. However, the taxation of church-owned businesses was endorsed whenever such activities were unrelated to religious work and were in competition with private businesses. It was suggested that preference for veterans of the military services when seeking government employment should be limited to only a few years after leaving the service. Favoritism of certain educational institutions in hiring government leaders was criticized. The party endorsed year-round Daylight Savings Time after considerable debate.

While defending freedom of the press, the platform condemned the news media for "sensationalizing a growing moral permissiveness." They were accused of creating the impression of being "approving and applauding onlookers." The nation's welfare system was described as being in a state of "disgraceful shambles." The party pointed with pride to its pioneering support of aid to the genuinely needy. But it stated: "The tragedy is that many who are truly deserving today are receiving insufficient aid." The platform rejected the guaranteed annual income as something that would "accelerate" the misdirection of funds rather than solve the problem. While the platform recognized the growing drug problem, it insisted by its facts and figures that alcohol remained the most serious social evil. In a special resolution, the party deplored the change of dates for national holidays to make longer weekends, characterizing it as "a sacrilege for the sake of commercial convenience."

Just prior to the convention, Hillsdale College awarded the party's national chairman an honorary doctoral degree in recognition of his long years of service to that institution. For the first time in the history of the party, a presidential standard-bearer was nominated for a third time in succession. E. Harold Munn, Sr. was nominated on the second ballot.

Four other candidates were presented to the convention, but those opposed to breaking the tradition of two nominations centered their support around Charles Wesley Ewing, a Michigan clergyman. One unusual feature was that Munn and Ewing each delivered the nominating speech for the other. Munn was nominated over Ewing on the second ballot, 31 to 19 after states had changed their votes. Only four votes separated the two before switches were made.

For vice president, the convention selected the youngest nominee in half a century. Marshall Uncapher of Hutchinson, Kansas was chosen on the first ballot over one opponent (30-22). As a sales representative for M. W. Hartman Manufacturing Company, he has been able to make many appearances on behalf of the party during his travels all over the country. He is a former school teacher and principal.

Following the convention, the National Committee chose Rev. Charles Wesley Ewing as its Chairman to succeed Dr. Munn. Earl F. Dodge was re-elected Executive Secretary. Rev. Ewing is nationally known as a temperance lecturer and as the author of the book **The Bible and Its Wines.** The Wichita convention also saw the formal organization of the Partisan Prohibition Historical Society to preserve the party's long heritage of achievement. There were fifteen charter members from eleven states.

The 1972 campaign opened with several discouraging obstacles. A whole new battery of repressive ballot laws had been enacted since the intensive third party activity of 1968. New barriers in three states where the party had been making progress precluded access to the ballots of these states. A defection in the Indiana leadership also ended chances of filing a ticket there for the first time since the party was founded. A federal court ruling threw the Prohibition Party and one other party off the ballot in Massachusetts, declaring a more lenient ballot law unconstitutional. The decision is being appealed. For the first time, the party is also challenging the California ballot laws in the state courts with a good chance of winning.

The party was cheered when an active partisan was elected to local office for the first time in several years. The party's national secretary was elected to a three-year term on the board of directors of a five-town school administrative district in eastern Maine. By virtue of the office, he is also a member of a twelve-township joint board for a school superintending union. The main issue in the election was preservation of neighborhood schools and his opposition to a busing plan.

The Prohibition Party faces three major challenges in 1972 as it enters the second century of its existence and its twenty-sixth presidential campaign.

I. THE DECLINE OF LOCAL GOVERNMENT IN RURAL AREAS.

While the number of local governments is declining steadily, there are still well over 150,000 units in existence, each with many offices to fill. Most are dominated by one major party. Often the two major parties divide territories between them and develop cozy arrangements by which neither will hurt the other's spheres of influence. In many of the smaller units, "dry" sentiment remains strong and voters often welcome competition from a third party where none exists from a major party.

Local elections of the past decade have continued to demonstrate that the Prohibition Party can still do well when good candidates are fielded. Preserving the moral and spiritual climate of rural America and the vitality of its local governments must be considered one of the major challenges. The accelerating dispersal of the population makes this even more imperative. Nor should it be assumed that people who move to the country are hostile to small-town values. Often they are uprooted from their old ties and open to the new approaches and concerns that the party can offer.

II. A CATALYTIC AGENT IN URBAN AND STATEWIDE CONTESTS.

It is no longer realistic to expect big election victories in complex urban societies and statewide elections. Yet, several times in the past decade the Prohibition Party has demonstrated the capacity of a small group of people to arouse public indignation and to raise the moral tone of a city's public life.

By capturing the balance of power in several state contests in the past decade, the Prohibition Party has continued to demonstrate that a few votes of a few morally alert citizens can matter very much to the victory or loss of a major party. To enter such contests with no hope of winning requires a special kind of courage and determination.

Few of the candidate's friends and neighbors understand what he is doing or why. Their reaction varies from silent pity, to open ridicule, to anger that stems from internal guilt for their own lack of response. But when candidates of such courage can be found, they continue to get a response that serves as a catalytic agent.

III. THE CHANGING CONDITIONS OF
PRESIDENTIAL CAMPAIGNING

It is vital for the Prohibition Party to continue running a national ticket as the rallying cry for the temperance movement. No other act draws more publicity and public consideration. The party's national campaigns and meetings serve as a means of interdenominational cooperation among Christians who belong to evangelistic churches that have been slow to cooperate in general. The party has been a stimulus to other temperance groups in pursuing their particular types of programs, helping to keep them from taking softer stands on moral issues.

But the party campaigns are a vehicle to reach people in ways that others cannot. There are millions of newly-enfranchised students in high schools and colleges. They are open and curious. Many are experimenting with drugs and other forms of moral permissiveness placed before them by a spiritually bankrupted social and political system. They will not listen to an old-fashioned temperance lecturer but they will listen to a candidate for office. In like manner, the news media will publicize the statements of a candidate when they will ignore a preacher or a lecturer. And so the Prohibition Party has called on preachers to become candidates.

But the party meets a new threat that must be faced. Legal barriers and astronomical costs in gaining the ballot make it impossible to be a bonafide candidate in an increasing number of states. This is not likely to change, but there is an alternative.

Presidential primaries are becoming less and less a party function, and more and more the first round of a general election. This year sees a sharp rise in the number of states where primaries are open to all voters regardless of party. The number of states where anyone's name may be entered by a simple decision of an election official is also increasing. This will probably have to be the forum of the future where the party can show its strength.

Many elections in recent years have revealed a large number of voters willing to vote for Prohibition candidates in contests that are "less vital" in the voters' minds. Candidates at the lower end of the ticket often poll many times the votes of those at the top. The party can expect to do better in presidential primaries and have considerably more influence on the campaigns. Of course, the party should continue to enter the general elections where it can. But it should consider entering contests in open-primary, easy-access states where the general election ballot is closed to the party.

People are often puzzled as to how and why the Prohibition Party has lasted so long. No other minor party has ever survived for anything like this length of time. And yet, it has always been so small and has had disasters befall it so many times that have ended other third parties in comparable situations. One must consider that some great moral imperative has given its partisans the strength to go on.

This author has been impressed and deeply moved by their blueprint of a Christian society. Indeed, it is startling how close the vision came to being realized. In the spirit of the ancient prophets, they called a nation to repent and to seek righteousness through the vehicle of a political party.

Theirs was never a happy or a pleasant task. Politicians like to find scapegoats on which to blame our troubles. But the partisan prophet, with humility and without gloating, must point out our own faults. Someone must hear the call for duty, to declare that the trouble lies with the sin of our own hearts. The healing and regenerating of a nation must come from a Power above us, not from the powers that we presume to be our own. It is that Power which the partisan prophets have strived to proclaim.

BIBLIOGRAPHY

Babson, Roger W., *Our Campaign for the Presidency in 1940*, National Prohibitionist, Chicago, 1941.

Bartlett, Irving H., *Wendell Phillips, Brahmin Radical*, Beacon Press, Boston, 1961.

Byrne, Frank L., *Prophet of Prohibition, Neal Dow and His Crusade*, State Historical Society of Wisconsin, Madison, 1961.

Colvin, D. Leigh, *Prohibition in the United States*, Columbia University Press, New York, 1926.

Daily Eastern Argus of Portland, Maine, newspaper articles on the 1900 and 1902 campaigns.

Dictionary of American Biography.

Dow, Frederick N., *Prohibition — Why, How, Then, Now,* Maine Woman's Christian Temperance Union, Portland, 1931.

Dow, Neal, *The Reminiscences of Neal Dow,* Evening Express Publishing Co., Portland, 1898.

Earhart, Mary, *Frances Willard, From Prayers to Politics,* University of Chicago Press, Chicago, 1944.

Fairfield, Roy P., *Sands, Spindles and Steeples: A History of Saco, Maine,* House of Falmouth, Portland, 1956.

Hamblen, Oberia, *My Brother, Stuart Hamblen,* Cowman Publications, Los Angeles, 1950.

James, George W., *Heroes of California,* Little, Brown and Co., Boston, 1910, pp. 45-55 (John Bidwell).

National Cyclopedia of American Biography.

National Prohibitionist, official organ of the Prohibition Party from 1933 through 1961.

National Statesman, official organ of the Prohibition Party from 1962 to the present.

Odegard, Peter H., *Pressure Politics: The Story of the Anti-Saloon League,* Columbia University Press, New York, 1928.

Ross, Ishbel, *Crusades and Crinolines, The Life and Times of Ellen Curtis Demorest and William Jennings Demorest,* Harper & Row, New York, 1963.

Sinclair, Andrew, *Prohibition, The Era of Excess,* Little, Brown and Co., Boston, 1962.

Taylor, Robert L., *Vessel of Wrath, The Life and Times of Carry Nation,* New American Library, New York, 1966.

Thayer, George, *Farther Shores of Politics,* Simon & Schuster, New York, 1967.

Who's Who in America, 1899-1972.

Woodbury, Nathan F., *Prohibition in Maine,* Maine Prohibition Committee, Auburn, 1920.

APPENDIX A

NATIONAL PROHIBITION CANDIDATES AND VOTES

Year	For President	For Vice President	Total Vote
1872	James Black Pennsylvania	John Russell Michigan	5,607
1876	Green Clay Smith Kentucky	Gideon T. Stewart Ohio	9,737
1880	Neal Dow Maine	Henry A. Thompson Ohio	10,304
1884	John P. St. John Kansas	William Daniel Maryland	153,128
1888	Clinton B. Fisk New Jersey	John A. Brooks Missouri	249,945
1892	John Bidwell California	James B. Cranfill Texas	271,058
1896	Joshua Levering Maryland	Hale Johnson Illinois	130,617
	(Bentley and Southgate)		(13,969)
1900	John G. Woolley Illinois	Henry B. Metcalf Rhode Island	209,469
1904	Silas C. Swallow Pennsylvania	George W. Carroll Texas	258,205
1908	Eugene W. Chafin Wisconsin	Aaron S. Watkins Ohio	253,231
1912	Eugene W. Chafin Wisconsin	Aaron S. Watkins Ohio	207,828
1916	J. Frank Hanly Indiana	Ira Landrith Tennessee	221,329
1920	Aaon S. Watkins Ohio	D. Leigh Colvin New York	195,923
1924	Herman P. Faris Missouri	Marie C. Brehm California	56,289
1928	William F. Varney New York	James A. Edgerton Virginia	20,106*
	(Hoover in California)		(14,394)
1932	William D. Upshaw Georgia	Frank S. Regan Illinois	81,869
1936	D. Leigh Colvin New York	Claude A. Watson California	37,847
1940	Roger W. Babson Massachusetts	Edgar V. Moorman Illinois	59,492
1944	Claude A. Watson California	Andrew Johnson Kentucky	74,758

1948	Claude A. Watson California	Dale H. Learn Pennsylvania	103,343
1952	Stuart Hamblen California	Enoch A. Holtwick Illinois	78,818
1956	Enoch A. Holtwick Illinois	Edwin M. Cooper California	41,937
1960	Rutherford L. Decker Missouri	E. Harold Munn, Sr. Michigan	46,239
1964	E. Harold Munn, Sr. Michigan	Mark R. Shaw Massachusetts	23,267
1968	E. Harold Munn, Sr. Michigan	Rolland E. Fisher Kansas	15,123
1972	E. Harold Munn, Sr. Michigan	Marshall E. Uncapher Kansas	

* The 1928 vote does not include 3,875 Penneylvania write-ins for Varney.
Most of the other figures include write-ins, absentees, and other votes
often excluded from official returns.

APPENDIX B
NATIONAL CONVENTION SITES

1869	Chicago, Illinois
1872	Columbus, Ohio
1876	Cleveland, Ohio
1880	Cleveland, Ohio
1884	Pittsburgh, Pennsylvania
1888	Indianapolis, Indiana
1892	Cincinnati, Ohio
1896	Pittsburgh, Pennsylvania
1900	Chicago, Illinois
1904	Indianapolis, Indiana
1908	Columbus, Ohio
1912	Atlantic City, New Jersey
1916	St. Paul, Minnesota
1920	Lincoln, Nebraska
1924	Columbus, Ohio
1928	Chicago, Illinois
1932	Indianapolis, Indiana
1936	Niagara Falls, New York
1940	Chicago, Illinois
1943	Indianapolis, Indiana
1947	Winona Lake, Indiana
1951	Indianapolis, Indiana
1955	Milford (Camp Mack), Indiana
1959	Winona Lake, Indiana
1963	St. Louis, Missouri
1967	Detroit, Michigan
1971	Wichita, Kansas

APPENDIX C

CHAIRMEN OF THE PROHIBITION NATIONAL COMMITTEE

1867-1972	John Russell, Michigan
1872-1876	Simeon B. Chase, Pennsylvania
1876-1880	James Black, Pennsylvania
1880-1884	Gideon T. Stewart, Ohio
1884-1887	John B. Finch, Nebraska
1887-1900	Samuel Dickie, Michigan
1900-1905	Oliver W. Stewart, Illinois
1905-1908	Charles R. Jones, Pennsylvania
1908-1924	Virgil G. Hinshaw, Oregon
1924-1925	B. E. P. Prugh, Pennsylvania
1925-1932	D. Leigh Colvin, New York
1932-1947	Edward E. Blake, Illinois
1947-1950	Virgil C. Finnell, Indiana
1950-1953	Gerald Overholt, Texas
1953-1955	Lowell H. Coate, California
1955-1971	E. Harold Munn, Sr., Michigan Earl F. Dodge, Massachusetts Co-Chairman, 1958-1962 Delmar D. Gibbons, Michigan Co-Chairman, 1963-1967 Earl F. Dodge, Michigan Executive Secretary, 1967-1971
1971-	Charles W. Ewing, Michigan Earl F. Dodge, Colorado Executive Secretary 1971-